Historical Sources on Slavery

CHET'LA SEBREE AND ELIZABETH SIRIMARCO

New York

Published in 2020 by Cavendish Square Publishing, LLC
243 5th Avenue, Suite 136, New York, NY 10016

First Edition

Website: cavendishsq.com

Library of Congress Cataloging-in-Publication Data

Names: Sebree, Chet'la. | Sirimarco, Elizabeth.
Title: Historical sources on slavery / Chet'la Sebree and Elizabeth Sirimarco.
Description: New York : Cavendish Square, 2020. |
Series: America's story | Includes glossary and index.
Identifiers: ISBN 9781502640864 (pbk.) | ISBN 9781502640871 (library bound) |
ISBN 9781502640888 (ebook)
Subjects: LCSH: Slavery--United States--History--Juvenile literature. |
African Americans--History--To 1863--Juvenile literature.
Classification: LCC E441.S46 2019 | DDC 306.3'620973--dc23

Editorial Director: David McNamara
Copy Editor: Nathan Heidelberger
Associate Art Director: Alan Sliwinski
Designer: Christina Schults
Production Coordinator: Karol Szymczuk
Photo Research: J8 Media

The photographs in this book are used by permission and through the courtesy of:
Cover, p 43 Everett Historical/Shutterstock.com, (background and used throughout) Foxstudio/Shutterstock.com; p. 4Library of Congress; p. 8 Susan Law Cain/Shutterstock.com; p. 13, 32, 80 Kean Collection/Getty Images; p. 16 Universal History Archive/UIG/Getty Images; p. 19 Société de la morale chrétienne/Wikimedia Commons/File:Dessin et coupes du navire négrier Le Brookes.jpg/Public Domain; p. 21 World History Archive/UIG/Getty images; p. 29 Jos. A. Beard/Wikimedia Commons/File:ValuableGangOfYoungNegroes1840.jpeg/Public Domain; p. 37 David Smart/Shutterstock.com; p. 44 Frederick M. Coffin (engraved by Nathaniel Orr)/Wikimedia Commons/File:Solomon Northup 001.jpg/Public Domain; p. 49 Fotosearch/Getty Images; p. 55 Historical Images Archive/Alamy Stock Photo; p. 60 Library of Congress; p. 64 Hulton Archive/Getty Images; p. 71 State Archives of North Carolina Raleigh, NC/Wikimedia Commons/File:Harriet Jacobs.jpg/Public Domain; p. 77 North Wind Picture Archives; p. , 91Stock Montage/Getty Images; p. 97 File:Ellen Craft escaped slave.jpg/Wikimedia Commons/File:Ellen Craft escaped slave.jpg/Public Domain; p. 98 Lanmas / Alamy Stock Photo; p 101 Hulton Archive/Getty Images; p. 106 Engraved by J.C. Buttre/Wikimedia Commons/File:Frederick Douglass as a younger man.jpg/Public Domain; p. 110 MPI/Getty Images; p. 112 Bettmann/Getty Images; p. 115 Missouri History Museum/Wikimedia Commons/File:Oil on Canvas Portrait of Dred Scott.jpg/Public Domain; p. 128 Alfred R. Waud/Library of Congress/Wikimedia Commons/File:Freedman bureau harpers cartoon.jpg/Public Domain; p. 131 Jack Delano/Library of Congress/File:JimCrowInDurhamNC.jpg/Public Domain.

Printed in the United States of America

CONTENTS

President Abraham Lincoln issued the Emancipation Proclamation, freeing all those enslaved in the Confederacy, in January 1863. The proclamation is a primary source.

Primary Sources

In the pages that follow, you will hear from many different people from a time in America's past. These selections will vary in length. Some are long, and others are short. You'll find many easy to understand at first reading, but some may require several readings. All the selections have one thing in common, however. They are primary sources. They are important to us because they are the core material for all historical investigation.

What Is a Primary Source?

The term "primary source" is the name historians give to the information that makes up the record of human existence. A primary source is "history" itself. Primary sources are evidence. They give historians the all-important clues they need to understand the past.

Perhaps you have read a detective story in which an investigator has to solve a mystery by piecing together bits of evidence that he or she uncovers. The detective makes deductions, or educated guesses based on the evidence, and solves the mystery once all the deductions point in a certain direction. Historians work in much the same way. Like detectives, they analyze data through careful reading and rereading. After much analysis, they draw conclusions about an event, a person, or an entire era. Different historians may analyze the same evidence and come to different conclusions. That is why there is often strong disagreement about an event.

Primary sources are also called documents. It is a rather dry word to describe what can be just about anything: an official speech by a government leader, an old map, an act of Congress, a letter, a diary entry, a newspaper article, a song, a poster, a cartoon, a photograph, or someone captured on tape or film.

By examining the following documents, you will be taking on the role of historian. Here is your chance to dive into a troubling era of American history: the 250 years of slavery. You will come to know the voices of the men and women who lived through this period. You will read the words of political leaders, abolitionists, rebels, and writers. Most important, you will also hear from those who were enslaved.

How to Read a Primary Source

Each document in this book deals with the history of slavery in America. Some of them are government documents. Others are excerpts, or selections, from the narratives and autobiographies of those who were themselves enslaved. All of the documents can help us learn about the time when slavery was legal in the United States.

The selections you will read may be difficult to understand at first. There will be a variety of styles, from very formal to quite informal. Don't let the writing put you off. Interpreting these kinds of documents is exactly the sort of work a historian does.

As you read each document, ask yourself some basic questions. Who is writing or speaking? Who is that person's intended audience? What is he or she trying to tell the audience? Is the message clearly expressed or is it implied, or stated indirectly? What words does the writer use to convey his or her message? Are the words emotional or neutral in tone? These are questions that can help you think critically about a primary source.

There are also some tools in each chapter to help you unpack these documents. Some terms and concepts you may not be familiar with have been explained in sidebars. Also, questions follow each of the documents to help you focus and think through the primary source you have just read. As you read each selection, you'll probably come up with many questions of your own. That's great! The work of a historian always leads to many, many questions. Some can be answered, while others will require more investigation.

IN CONGRESS, JULY 4, 1776.

…e unanimous Declaration of the thirteen united States of Ame…

The Declaration of Independence officially established the United States of America in 1776.

Introduction

Slavery in America

Thomas Jefferson wrote the Declaration of Independence in 1776. In it, he wrote "that all men are created equal, that they are endowed by their Creator with certain unalienable Rights." In other words, he wrote that all men are alike and have rights that cannot be taken from them for any reason. Some of these rights include "Life, Liberty and the pursuit of Happiness." These words are the foundation on which the United States was built in a figurative sense. In a more literal sense, the country was built by enslaved Africans. These people were owned, not treated equally, and not given these "unalienable Rights."

Servitude in Colonial America

Slavery was not always a central part of the American landscape. In 1619, English pirates brought twenty Africans to Jamestown, Virginia, to be sold into slavery. These Africans were originally aboard a Portuguese slave ship on its way to Mexico from Angola. They were the first Africans to arrive in England's North American colonies for the purpose of slave labor. It was not until the end of the seventeenth century that Africans became the dominant source of labor in colonial America.

At first, colonists relied more on indentured servants from England and other parts of Europe. These were people who agreed to four to seven years of servitude in exchange for passage to the New World. These contract servants received food, shelter, and clothing during their term of service. Like enslaved Africans, indentured servants could be bought and sold. Unlike those who were enslaved, indentured servants were free once they completed their contracts. Eventually, colonists began to move away from indentured servitude because fewer people were willing to enter into the contracts. This was partially because more jobs were available in England.

Colonists still needed laborers, so they tried to force Native Americans into slave labor. However, for a variety of reasons, Natives were never a major part of the workforce. For one, their knowledge of the land made it easier for them to escape slavery. One of the biggest reasons, however, was that they simply didn't survive the European invasion. Diseases, especially smallpox, devastated the Natives. The number of Native Americans alive today is only a tiny fraction of what their population had been in the fifteenth century, before the arrival of Europeans.

The decrease in indentured servants combined with the inability to use Native Americans as enslaved laborers led to a labor crisis in the colonies. It was one that came at an inconvenient time.

The Transition to Slave Labor

In the Southern colonies, agriculture—particularly the raising of crops such as tobacco and cotton—was beginning to make a small number of planters very wealthy. This success required significant manpower. Looking for other sources of labor, the colonists turned to enslaved Africans. Their farming skills made them highly valued workers. They also seemed well adapted to the intense heat and humidity of the South, given the climates in some regions of Africa.

Although the majority of people who were enslaved lived in the Southern colonies, slavery was not restricted to that region. In 1690, for example, one out of every nine families in Boston owned an African. The proportion was even higher in New York City. Ultimately, though, geography, revolutions, and inventions would change the landscape of slavery in colonial America.

The Tides of Change

Two major revolutions changed the way slavery would progress in America. First, the Industrial Revolution, which started in the 1760s, brought change to the colonial American landscape. It introduced technology that converted the North to a manufacturing economy. The North depended on machinery and the paid labor of the working class to produce goods.

Second, the spirit of the American Revolution inspired some citizens of the North to see slavery as inconsistent with the values of the young nation. In 1777, Vermont became the first state to abolish slavery. Pennsylvania followed three years later with a law that gradually freed those enslaved. For instance, it prohibited the importation of new enslaved Africans. However, those already enslaved would remain enslaved. Over the next twenty years, the Northern states made arrangements for the emancipation, or formal freedom, of their enslaved laborers. Abolitionist societies, or organizations focused on the end of slavery, were organized throughout the region.

Additionally, the North generally had small, independent farms. Being smaller, these farms did not rely as heavily on agricultural laborers. Slavery in the South, however, continued to grow as the economy became more and more reliant on agriculture. Unlike the North, the South was made up of large plantations that needed to be worked by many laborers. In the South, slavery had a greater effect on the economy. This would be especially true after the invention of the cotton gin, a machine that separates cotton from its seeds.

Invented in 1793 by Eli Whitney, the cotton gin had a tremendous impact on the production of cotton in the South and ultimately on the practice of slavery. Cleaning the seeds from cotton by hand was a difficult and time-consuming job. Before Whitney's invention, a worker could manage to clean only about 1 pound (0.45 kilograms) of cotton a day. With the cotton gin and a few laborers, it became possible to clean 50 pounds (22.7 kg) a day. What once took a whole crew of workers a full day to accomplish could now be done in minutes.

Whitney's cotton gin revived the sagging Southern economy. Demand for cotton increased enormously. Southern plantation owners used enslaved laborers to plant more and more fields of the profitable crop. They also used enslaved laborers to pick and collect the cotton. This work was even more unpleasant than cleaning it by hand. Although the young country had seen an influx of immigrants willing to work for low wages, few were willing to take on this disagreeable job. Thus, as the rest of the nation turned away from slave labor, Southerners increasingly grew to rely on it.

Still, Northern states, and European nations as well, played significant roles in the system of slavery. They provided markets where the South sold its cotton and tobacco. These crops were grown and harvested through the backbreaking work of enslaved laborers. Equally significant, the majority of slave traders, or merchants who transported captive Africans from their homeland to the New World, were European. What's more, while the institution of slavery may have faded in the North, Northerners did not uniformly support emancipation or even equal rights for people of African descent. They were not immune to racism, either.

The way in which Eli Whitney's cotton gin revolutionized the cotton industry would change not only the nature of slavery but also the course of US history.

While black people in the North were free, they still did not enjoy the same rights and privileges as white citizens did.

The American Civil War

Even though the North benefited from slavery, an imaginary boundary began to separate North from South. Slavery divided the nation, both literally and figuratively. By the middle of the nineteenth century, it had become an explosive political issue. The abolitionists were gaining momentum with the help of such articulate speakers as William Lloyd Garrison and Frederick Douglass. They were convincing more and more people that slavery was an evil that threatened to destroy the nation. Slaveholders came up with incredible arguments to defend their position. For instance, some cited the Bible or fake science as evidence of the inferiority of Africans.

At the same time, many Northern politicians began to support "free soil." This was the idea that slavery be made illegal in any new territory added to the young country as it expanded westward. This concept led to a short-lived political party, the Free-Soil Party (1848–1854). For their part, most Southerners believed that such a law would be unconstitutional. They cited states' rights. It is the idea that each individual state, rather than the federal government, had the right to make decisions about certain issues, such as slavery, that affected life within its borders. States' rights are protected by the Tenth Amendment to the Constitution.

The troubled state of the Union reached a critical point with Abraham Lincoln's election to the presidency in 1860. Lincoln was a member of the Republican Party, which was founded in 1854 and absorbed many people in the Free-Soil Party. Most early Republicans believed that the nation's interests should take priority over those of the individual states. Many were free soil advocates who opposed the spread of slavery. Southerners saw Lincoln's election as the beginning of the end of slavery and their world as they knew it.

Determined to maintain their way of life, eleven Southern states seceded, or formally withdrew, from the Union. They formed the Confederate States of America. In the Confederate states, slavery would remain legal until 1863, when Lincoln's Emancipation Proclamation took effect. This presidential order freed those enslaved in the Confederacy, though some would remain enslaved until the end of the war. Additionally, people remained enslaved in some states that had remained part of the Union. The Thirteenth Amendment, which outlawed slavery in all states and territories, was finally passed in 1865 by Congress. The South lost the Civil War that same year.

Many enslaved Africans were forced to march long distances before boarding ships bound for slave auctions in the United States.

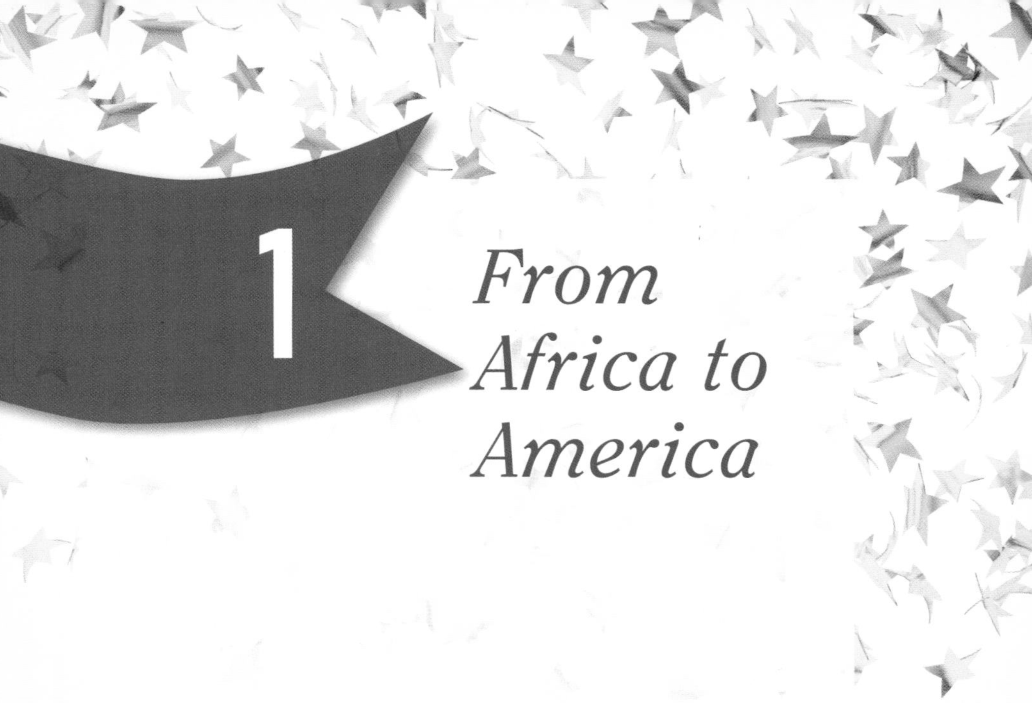

1 From Africa to America

Slavery existed in Africa long before the arrival of the Europeans. There was already an established East African slave trade, which supplied enslaved people to the Arab world, as well as a trans-Saharan slave trade between Northern and sub-Saharan Africa. Africans generally accepted the institution of slavery. However, it was viewed differently.

Domestic Slavery in Africa

The treatment of slaves in Africa was generally much more humane than it would be in the Americas. Enslaved Africans in the African slavery system often retained some rights. The system may have looked more like indentured servitude, some historians believe. As one observer noted, "They are remarkably kind to, and careful of their slaves … whom they treat with respect, and whom they will not suffer to be ill-used." By contrast, the observer explained,

"Europeans … treat [the slaves] as if they were a lower order of creatures, and abuse them in the most shocking manner."

The continent of Africa has a diverse population, made up of many different peoples. Generally, African slave traders did not sell people from their own tribe or homeland. Until Europeans entered the picture, the majority of the people who were enslaved were prisoners of war, or villagers captured during raids. Sometimes leaders enslaved their own subjects, usually as punishment for unpaid debts or criminal acts. Occasionally, they sold their people into slavery during times of drought and famine.

The Demands of the New World

Beginning in the late seventeenth century, the demand for enslaved laborers in the New World exploded, as did the money that could be made in the slave trade. This changed things dramatically for Africans on many parts of the continent. Captives could now be sent thousands of miles from their homes, not to another village within real or imagined reach of one's home and loved ones. Innocent people living in unprotected villages, such as young children, women, men, and even the elderly, were increasingly vulnerable to unprovoked attacks and kidnappings. Spurred by greed or hoping to protect their own, some rulers worked hand in hand with traders. Africans were increasingly made captive for minor debts, petty crimes, and even religious beliefs.

The Journey of Enslaved Africans

Once captured, enslaved people were chained together and forced to march, often barefoot and for hundreds of miles, to the western coast of Africa. European merchants, primarily from England, France, and Portugal, had set up trading posts on the coast. Many captives died during this journey. Skeletons were said to litter the roadside along the routes that the traders used. In exchange for

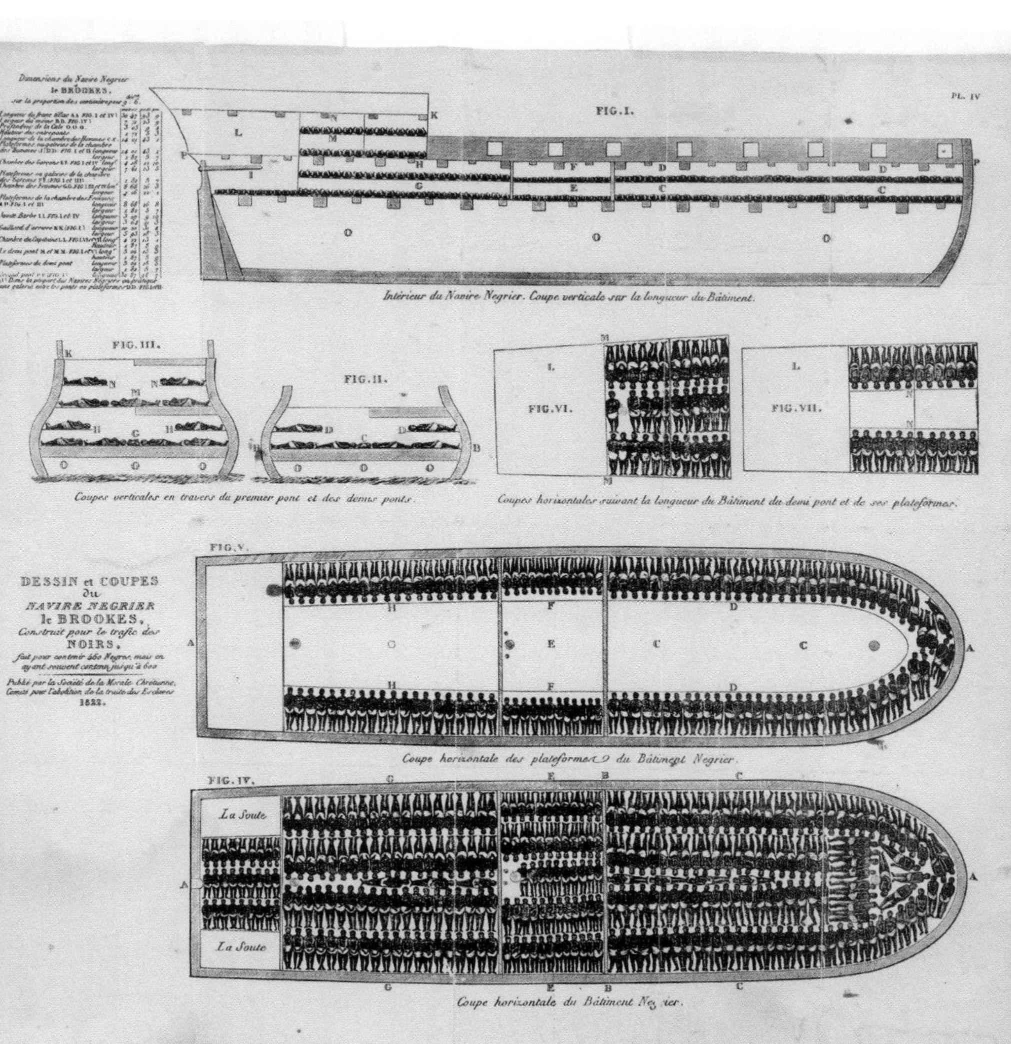

This image depicts how enslaved Africans were packed into cargo holds of ships in close proximity to each other. They usually had little room to even sit upright.

human beings, European traders offered items such as firearms, gold, shells, alcohol, and beads.

After purchase, European slave traders prepared the enslaved Africans for the second leg of their journey. They loaded them into the hold, or the part of a ship meant for cargo, of a slave ship bound for the New World. They shackled the Africans in dark, cramped quarters without fresh air. The trip across the Atlantic Ocean is known as the Middle Passage. It claimed a huge number of lives. A quarter of the captured Africans easily might die of malnutrition and disease during the journey. Some of the captives committed suicide to escape the ships' inhumane conditions and slavery.

For those who made it to the New World, the final leg of the journey involved their sale. As the Africans stood in fear and confusion, New World buyers inspected them like livestock. Once purchased, most slaves were separated from any friends or family members who had made the journey with them.

From the 1520s through the 1860s, Europeans forced an estimated ten to twelve million Africans from their homelands. About six hundred thousand of these captives ended up in the thirteen colonies, and later the United States. Many more never made it that far. From 10 to 15 percent of captives died on the march to the coast. More died while waiting for weeks on European slave ships before the transatlantic voyage. Some 15 to 25 percent more Africans died during the Middle Passage.

The following selections offer accounts of the horrific journey from Africa to America, some from those who survived the journey, and from capture to sale.

Olaudah Equiano's Story of His Capture

Olaudah Equiano was among the first of many former slaves to write about their experiences. Born in 1745, in what is now southeastern Nigeria, Equiano was the son of a chief, who himself owned slaves. Equiano was kidnapped as a young boy and lived as a slave in two African villages before European slave traders sent him to the Americas. Later sold to a merchant in the Caribbean, Equiano was given a position of responsibility that allowed him to earn a small amount of money for himself. In 1766, he was able to purchase his freedom.

Equiano moved to England, where he wrote and published *The Interesting Narrative of the Life of Olaudah Equiano, or Gustavus Vassa*. Gustavus Vassa was the name given to Equiano by one of his masters. The book was widely read in both England and the United States. In the following passage, Equiano recalls his capture at the age of eleven.

> One day, when all our people were gone out to their works as usual, and only I and my dear sister were left to mind the house, two men and a woman got over our walls, and in a moment seized us both; and, without giving us time to cry out, or make resistance, they stopped our mouths, and ran off with us into the nearest wood. Here they tied our hands, and continued to carry us as far as they could, till night came on, when we reached a small house, where the robbers halted for refreshment, and spent the night. We were then unbound; but were unable to

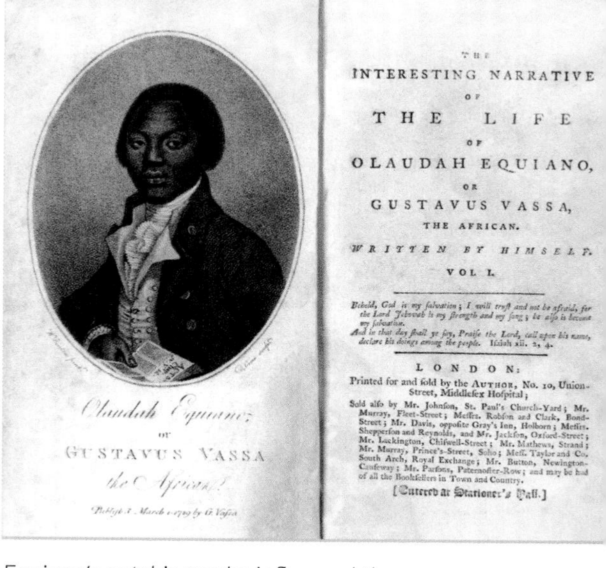

Olaudah Equiano; or GUSTAVUS VASSA *the African.*

THE INTERESTING NARRATIVE OF THE LIFE OF OLAUDAH EQUIANO, OR GUSTAVUS VASSA, THE AFRICAN.

WRITTEN BY HIMSELF.

VOL I.

Behold, God is my ſalvation; I will truſt and not be afraid, for the Lord Jehovah is my ſtrength and my ſong; he alſo is become my ſalvation.
And in that day ſhall ye ſay, Praiſe the Lord, call upon his name, declare his doings among the people. Iſaiah xii. 2, 4.

LONDON:

Printed for and ſold by the AUTHOR, No. 10, Union-Street, Middleſex Hoſpital;

Sold alſo by Mr. Johnſon, St. Paul's Church-Yard; Mr. Murray, Fleet-Street; Meſſrs. Robſon and Clark, Bond-Street; Mr. Davis, oppoſite Gray's Inn, Holborn; Meſſrs. Shepperſon and Reynolds, and Mr. Jackſon, Oxford-Street; Mr. Lackington, Chiſwell-Street; Mr. Mathews, Strand; Mr. Murray, Prince's-Street, Soho; Meſſ. Taylor and Co. South Arch, Royal Exchange; Mr. Button, Newington-Cauſeway; Mr. Parſons, Paternoſter-Row; and may be had of all the Bookſellers in Town and Country.

[Entered at Stationer's Hall.]

Equiano's autobiography influenced the abolishment of slavery in the United Kingdom and British colonies.

take any food; and, being quite overpowered by fatigue and grief,. our only relief was some sleep, which allayed our misfortune for a short time. The next morning we left the house and continued traveling all the day … I discovered some people at a distance, on which I began to cry out for their assistance; but my cries had no other effect than to make them tie me faster, and stop my mouth, and then they put me into a large sack. They also stopped my sister's mouth, and tied her hands; and in this manner we proceeded till we were out of the sight of these people.—When we went to rest the following night they offered us some victuals; but we refused them; and the only comfort we had was in being in one another's arms all that night, and bathing each other with our tears. But, alas! we were soon deprived of even the smallest comfort of weeping together. The next day proved a day of greater sorrow than I had yet experienced: for my sister and I were then separated, while we lay clasped in each other's arms. It was in vain that we besought them not to part us; she was torn from me, and immediately carried away.

—From Vincent Carretta, ed., *The Interesting Narrative of the Life of Olaudah Equiano, or Gustavus Vassa, the African. Written by Himself* (New York: Penguin Classics, 2003).

CONSIDER THIS

1. Why might the traders have chosen to kidnap children rather than adults?
2. Why do you think Equiano's family couldn't find him?

KEY TERMS AND CONCEPTS

From Olaudah Equiano's narrative:
allay To relieve or lessen.
besought The past tense of "to beseech." In other words, to beg.
victuals Food.

From Mahommah G. Baquaqua's account:
efface To erase.
noisome Offensive to the senses, especially the sense of smell.
refractory Disobedient.
wretch An unfortunate individual.

"The Noisome Hold": The Horrors of the Middle Passage

A former slave named Mahommah G. Baquaqua was among the millions of people who experienced the misery of the Middle Passage. Baquaqua was born in the city of Zoogoo in central Africa, around 1830. Captured and sold into slavery, he was transported first to Brazil and then the United States, where he was finally able to escape from slavery. In 1854, he told his life story to Samuel Moore, who published the account. The story includes a firsthand description of what it was like in the hold of a slave ship.

> Its horrors, ah! who can describe? None can so truly depict its horrors as the poor unfortunate, miserable wretch that has been confined within its portals ...

We were thrust into the hold of the vessel in a state of nudity, the males being crammed on one side and the females on the other; the hold was so low that we could not stand up, but were obliged to crouch upon the floor or sit down; day and night were the same to us, sleep being denied as from the confined position of our bodies, and we became desperate through suffering and fatigue.

Oh! the loathsomeness and filth of that horrible place will never be effaced from my memory; nay, as long as memory holds her seat in this distracted brain, will I remember that. My heart even at this day, sickens at the thought of it.

Let those humane individuals, who are in favor of slavery, only allow themselves to take the slave's position in the noisome hold of a slave ship, just for one trip from Africa to America, and without going into the horrors of slavery further than this, if they do not come out thorough-going abolitionists, then I have no more to say in favor of abolition ... I imagine there can be but one place more horrible in all creation than the hold of a slave ship, and that place is where slaveholders ... are the most likely to find themselves some day ...

The only food we had during the voyage was corn soaked and boiled. I cannot tell how long we were thus confined, but it seemed a very long while. We suffered very much for want of water, but was denied all we needed. A pint a day was all that was allowed, and no more; and a great many slaves died upon the passage. There was one poor fellow became so very desperate for want of water, that he attempted to snatch a knife from the white man who brought in the water, when he was taken up on deck and I never knew what became of him. I supposed he was thrown overboard.

When any one of us became refractory, his flesh was cut with a knife, and pepper or vinegar was rubbed in to make him peaceable (!) I suffered, and so did the rest of us, very much from sea sickness at first, but that did not cause our brutal owners any trouble. Our sufferings were our own, we had no one to share our troubles, none to care for us, or even to speak a word of comfort to us. Some were thrown overboard before breath was out of their bodies; when it was thought any would not live, they were got rid of in that way. Only twice during the voyage were we allowed to go on deck to wash ourselves—once whilst at sea, and again just before going into port.

—From Mahommah G. Baquaqua and Samuel Moore, *Biography of Mahommah G. Baquaqua, a Native of Zoogoo, in the Interior of Africa* (Detroit, MI: Geo. P. Pomeroy & Co., 1854).

CONSIDER THIS

1. Baquaqua suggests that there is only one place worse than the hold of a slave ship. Where do you think this is?
2. Why do you think those who were enslaved were allowed to wash before going to port?

"The Sorrows of Yamba": From Freedom to Slavery

"The Sorrows of Yamba" tells the story of an African woman kidnapped and then sold into slavery. It is often attributed to the British poet Hannah More (1745–1833). She was a tireless supporter of the abolitionist movement. More was the editor of a series of inexpensive publications called the *Cheap Repository Tracts*. They were designed for moral and religious instruction. More may or may not have been the author of "The Sorrows of Yamba." She may have simply published the poem for another writer, perhaps even a former slave. The work first appeared in England in 1795 and was published in the United States in 1805. The following excerpt offers a heartbreaking image of an African mother's grief.

"In St. Lucie's distant Isle,
Still with Afric's love I burn;
Parted many a thousand mile,
Never, never to return.

Come, kind death! and give me rest,
Yamba has no friend [but] thee;
Thou can'st ease my throbbing breast,
Thou can'st set the Prisoner free.

Down my cheeks the tears are dripping,
Broken is my heart with grief;
Mangled my poor flesh with whipping,
Come kind death! and bring relief.

Born on Afric's Golden Coast,
Once I was as blest as you;
Parents tender I could boast,
Husband dear, and children too.

FROM AFRICA TO AMERICA

Whity Man he came from far,
Sailing o'er the briny flood,
Who, with help of British Tar,
Buys up human flesh and blood.

With the Baby at my breast;
(Other two were sleeping by)
In my Hut I sat at rest
With no thought of danger nigh.

From the bush at even tide
Rush'd the fierce man-stealing Crew;
Seiz'd the Children by my side,
Seiz'd the wretched Yamba too.

Then for love of filthy Gold,
Strait they bore me to the sea;
Cramm'd me down a Slave-ship's hold,
Where were Hundreds stow'd like me.

Naked on the platform lying,
Now we cross the tumbling wave;
Shrieking, sickening, fainting, dying,
Deed of shame for Britons brave.

...

I in groaning pass'd the night,
And did roll my aching head;
At the break of morning light,
My poor Child was cold and dead.

Happy, happy there she lies!
Thou shalt feel the lash no more.

KEY TERMS AND CONCEPTS

From "The Sorrows of Yamba":

briny Salty.

nigh Near.

stinted Limited; of an inadequate amount.

tar A sailor.

From the slave auction broadside:

allowed Thought.

likeliest The most promising.

parcel A selection of enslaved Africans.

Thus full many a Negro dies,
Ere we reach the destin'd shore.

Driven like Cattle to a fair,
See they sell us young and old;
Child from Mother too they tear,
All for love of filthy Gold.

I was sold to Massa hard,
Some have Massas kind and good;
And again my back was scarr'd
Bad and stinted was my food.

Poor and wounded, faint and sick,
All exposs'd to burning sky,

1840

VALUABLE GANG OF YOUNG
NEGROES

By JOS. A. BEARD.

Will be sold at Auction,
ON WEDNESDAY, 25TH INST.
At 12 o'clock, at Banks' Arcade,
17 Valuable Young Negroes,
Men and Women, Field Hands.
Sold for no fault; with the best
city guarantees.

Sale Positive
and without reserve!
TERMS CASH.
New Orleans, March 24, 1840.

Broadsides like this one advertised slave auctions. Field hands were enslaved people who were responsible for planting and harvesting crops on plantations.

Massa bids me grass to pick,
And now I am near to die ..."

—From Hannah More (attributed), "The Sorrows of Yamba, or The Negro Woman's Lamentation." Reprinted in Addison Wesley Longman, ed., *The Longman Anthology of British Literature Vol. 2A, The Romantics and Their Contemporaries* (Upper Saddle River, NJ: Addison Wesley Longman, 1999).

CONSIDER THIS

1. How does Yamba feel about death? How would she have compared it to slavery?
2. Yamba's children were also kidnapped. What happened to them?

The Promise of Strong Slaves

The terrible conditions under which the African captives were transported helped make health concerns important to traders and slave owners alike. One infected individual could cause an epidemic, or a widespread occurrence of a particular disease. This epidemic would have serious consequences to plantation life.

To lessen the risks, newly arrived enslaved Africans were often quarantined, or put in isolation, for a period of time before being put up for auction. Other measures, such as cleaning or fumigating the ships, might also be taken. In the following broadside, or large printed advertisement, merchants reassure potential buyers at an upcoming auction that the enslaved Africans are free from smallpox.

CHARLESTOWN, April 27, 1769

TO BE SOLD,

On Wednesday the Tenth Day of
May next,

A CHOICE CARGO OF
Two Hundred & Fifty
NEGROES:

ARRIVED in the Ship
Countess of Sussex, Thomas Davies,

Master, directly from Gambia, by
JOHN CHAPMAN, & Co.

THIS is the Vessel that had the Small-Pox on Board at the Time of her Arrival the 31st of March last: Every necessary Precaution hath since been taken to cleanse both Ship and Cargo thoroughly, so that those who may be inclined to purchase need not be under the least Apprehension of Danger from Infliction.

The NEGROES are allowed to be the likeliest Parcel that have been imported this Season.

—From broadside of April 27, 1769, Charleston, South Carolina. Worchester, MA: American Antiquarian Society.

CONSIDER THIS

1. What emotions does this broadside stir in you? What thoughts does it evoke?
2. How do you think eighteenth-century slaveholders rationalized what they were doing?

Just the Beginning

As horrific as the journey was from capture to sale, still more horrors awaited enslaved Africans upon their arrival in America. Initially, in the American colonies, there were no set rules about the rights of enslaved people or how slave owners could treat them. It was new territory. For instance, in those early days, it was unclear whether someone who was enslaved could ever earn his or her freedom, or whether a child born to enslaved parents would also be enslaved. As the practice of slavery spread, the colonists began to create laws to protect their interest in continuing the institution.

This image depicts early enslaved Africans being examined by slave traders in Jamestown, Virginia.

2 The Legality of Slavery

As slavery spread, so, too, did the variety of laws that controlled the enslaved Africans and protected the slaveholders. These laws touched on every aspect of slaves' lives, often barring them from marrying, practicing religion, or learning to read and write. Laws also governed the harshness of punishment that the enslaved Africans could face, for everything from minor infractions such as disobedience to the larger crime of trying to escape. Chief among these were laws stating that, unlike indentured servants, these Africans would be enslaved for life, with little or no chance for freedom.

Slave Status in Virginia

In 1705, the lawmaking body in Virginia created a law that confirmed an enslaved person's status as chattel, or personal property. Soon, similar laws would be passed in other colonies as well.

> Be it enacted, by the governor, council and burgesses of this present general assembly, and it is hereby enacted by the authority of the same; That from and after the passing of this act, all negro, mulatto, and Indian slaves ... shall be held, taken, and adjudged, to be real estate ... and shall descend unto the heirs and widows of persons departing this life, according to the manner and custom of land of inheritance.
>
> —From William Waller Hening, October 1705, 4th Anne, Chap XXIII, 3.333, in *The Statutes at Large; Being a Collection of all the Laws of Virginia, from the First Session of the Legislature in the Year 1619*, Vol. 1 (New York: R & W & G. Bartow, 1823).

CONSIDER THIS

1. Consider what the term real estate usually means. What is the significance of calling a human being "real estate"?
2. According to this law, what happens to an enslaved person upon the death of his or her owner?

The South Carolina Slave Code

The Negro Law of 1740, also known as the South Carolina Slave Code, was enacted after a series of slave revolts in the 1730s. The law applied to all "people of color" who were enslaved, including Native Americans and those of mixed race. The law declared that all people enslaved in the colony of South Carolina were "forever and hereafter slaves." The code prohibited enslaved individuals from learning to read, write, or raise livestock. Additionally, it outlined strict punishments for slaves. The law

KEY TERMS AND CONCEPTS

From the Virginia law related to slaves' status:
adjudge To judge; or to determine by law.
burgesses Member of the governing body.
enact To make into law.
mulatto A person of mixed black and white ancestry.

From the Negro Law of 1740:
insurrection Rebellion or revolt.
pounds The currency of England used in the thirteen colonies. One pound in the mid-1740s would be equivalent to about $230 in 2018.
Province Colony.
put irons on To shackle.
switch A slender tree branch.

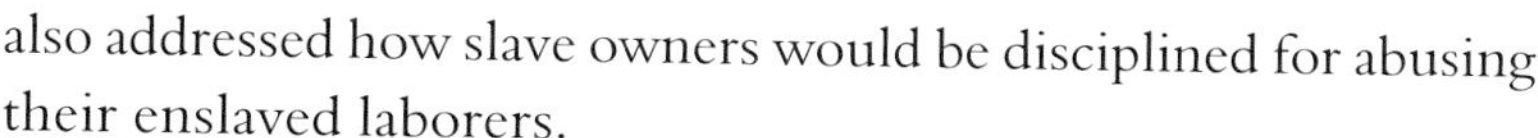

also addressed how slave owners would be disciplined for abusing their enslaved laborers.

> If any slave in this Province shall commit any crime or offence whatsoever, which by the laws of England, or of this Province, now in force, is or has been made felony … every such slave, being duly convicted according to the directions of this act, shall suffer death …
>
> Any slave who shall be guilty of homicide of any sort upon any white person, except by misadventure, or

in defence of his master ... shall upon conviction thereof as aforesaid, suffer death. And every slave who shall raise or attempt to raise an insurrection in this Province ... shall upon conviction as aforesaid, suffer death ...

Be it enacted, that if any person shall wilfully murder his own slave, or the slaves of any other person, every such person shall, upon conviction thereof, forfeit and pay the sum of seven hundred pounds ...

If any person shall, on a sudden heat or passion, or by undue correction, kill his own slave, or the slave of any other person, he shall forfeit the sum of three hundred and fifty pounds ...

In case any person shall wilfully cut out the tongue, put out the eye, castrate, or cruelly scald, burn, or deprive any slave of any limb or member, or shall inflict any other cruel punishment, other than by whipping, or beating with a horsewhip, cowskin, switch, or small stick, or by putting irons on, or confining or imprisoning such slave, every such person shall, for every such offense, forfeit the sum of one hundred pounds, current money.

—Cited by William Goodell, *The American Slave Code in Theory and Practice: Its Distinctive Features Shown by Its Statutes, Judicial Decisions, and Illustrative Facts* (New York: American and Foreign Anti-Slavery Society, 1853).

CONSIDER THIS

1. The law describes two penalties for murdering an enslaved individual. What is the difference between them?
2. Consider the punishment an enslaved person would receive for murdering a white person versus that which a slave owner would receive for murdering his slave or someone else's. Why do you think the penalties were so different? Whom were the laws protecting?
3. Is there any case in which an enslaved person would not be put to death for killing a white person?

The Founding Fathers Approve Slavery

The existence of slavery in a young nation founded on democratic principles seems like a contradiction to us today. However, many of the Founding Fathers—like Thomas Jefferson, George

The US Constitution established the foundational laws and system of government of the United States.

Washington, and Benjamin Franklin—were slave owners at some point in their lives.

So, when the Founding Fathers drew up the Constitution in 1787, did they have anything to say about slavery? Although the words "slave" and "slavery" are never mentioned in the document, the writers of the Constitution acknowledged the institution. Consider the following passages from the document and how they relate to slavery.

> Article I, Section 2
> Clause 3: Representatives and direct Taxes shall be apportioned among the several States ... according to their respective Numbers which shall be determined by adding to the whole Number of free Persons, including those bound to Service for a Term of Years, and excluding Indians not taxed, three fifths of all other Persons.
>
> Article I, Section 9
> Clause 1: The Migration or Importation of such Persons as any of the States now existing shall think proper to admit, shall not be prohibited by the Congress prior to the Year one thousand eight hundred and eight, but a Tax or duty may be imposed on such Importation, not exceeding ten dollars for each Person.
>
> Article IV, Section 2
> Clause 3: No Person held to Service or Labour in one State, under the Laws thereof, escaping into another, shall, in Consequence of any Law or Regulation therein, be discharged from such Service or Labour, but shall be delivered up on Claim of the Party to whom such Service or Labour may be due.

KEY TERMS AND CONCEPTS

From the US Constitution:

according to their respective Numbers According to the state's population.

apportioned Divided.

three fifths The idea that enslaved individuals were seen as three-fifths of a person in population terms.

From William Goodell's critique of slavery:

annual produce The crops grown on a piece of land over the course of a year.

brood mare A female horse used for breeding.

Henry Clay A congressman turned senator who eventually developed a negative view of slavery, though he was a slave owner his entire life.

hereditary transmission The idea that slavery would be passed down from one generation to the next.

Mr. Gholson Thomas Gholson Jr., a member of the Virginia General Assembly and later a US congressman.

perpetuity The state of lasting forever.

sanction Approval or permission.

—From the Constitution of the United States, adopted by a convention of the States on September 17, 1787.

CONSIDER THIS

1. The first passage says that the states will be taxed according to how many people reside within them. Does an enslaved individual count as a person in the population of a state?
2. Why do you think the Founding Fathers made it so that slavery couldn't be outlawed until 1808?
3. According to the last passage, if an enslaved person escaped to a state where slavery was illegal, would he or she be free?

A Child Follows "The Condition of the Mother"

Many slave owners argued that because slavery was legal, there was nothing wrong with them owning people. In 1853, a New York minister and abolitionist named William Goodell wrote *The American Slave Code in Theory and Practice* to disprove this belief.

Goodell argued that the laws protecting slavery should not be respected because slavery was essentially immoral, an act against God. In the following passage, Goodell describes a feature common to all the slave codes, one that ensured the continuation of slavery with each generation.

> Slaves being held as Property, like other domestic animals, their Offspring are held as Property, in perpetuity, in the same manner …
>
> In Maryland, "All negroes and other slaves, already imported or hereafter to be imported into this

province, and all children, now born or hereafter to be born of such negroes and slaves, shall be slaves during their natural lives." ...

Similar in Georgia ... And in Mississippi ... And in Virginia ... And in Kentucky ... And in Louisiana ... In all these laws it is laid down that the child follows the condition of the mother, whoever the father may be! The same usage, whether with or without written law, prevails in all our slave States; and under its sanction, the slave "owner" very frequently holds and sells his own children as "property," though sometimes as white as himself.

"That is property which the law declares TO BE property. Two hundred years of legislation have sanctified and sanctioned negro slaves as property." (HENRY CLAY; Speech, U.S. Senate, 1839.)

So also Mr. Gholson, in the Legislature of Virginia: "The owner of land has a reasonable right to its annual produce, the owner of brood mares to their products, and the owner of female slaves to their increase [offspring]."

Thus the perpetuity of slavery grows out of its hereditary transmission ... The duty of a future liberation would imply the unlawfulness of present possession. Intelligent slaveholders, perceiving this, are careful to fortify their present claims upon human chattels, by enactments seeking the perpetuity of the system.

—From William Goodell, "The Relation Hereditary and Perpetual," in *The American Slave Code in Theory and Practice: Its Distinctive Features Shown by Its Statutes, Judicial Decisions, and Illustrative Facts* (New York: American and Foreign Anti-Slavery Society, 1853).

CONSIDER THIS

1. Why do these laws apply to children born to enslaved women but say nothing about the fathers of the children?
2. To what does the Virginia legislator Mr. Gholson compare enslaved children?
3. Carefully consider the following sentence: "The duty of a future liberation would imply the unlawfulness of present possession." What does Goodell mean by this?

The End to the US Slave Trade

As mentioned before, Thomas Jefferson was one of the Founding Fathers who owned enslaved Africans. Jefferson recognized that slavery was a problem in the new nation, one that would only grow more dangerous as years passed. However, Jefferson himself never freed the majority of the people he owned. Additionally, he did not believe in racial equality.

Still, Jefferson tried several times to enact laws that would change the landscape of slavery in both Virginia and in the country. For instance, when writing the Declaration of Independence, Jefferson included a section condemning King George III of England for his support of slavery through the slave trade. Congress decided to eliminate the section when Georgia and South Carolina protested. Perhaps most important, Jefferson signed "An Act to Prohibit the Importation of Slaves" into law in 1807, while he was

Thomas Jefferson, Founding Father and third US president, signed into law an act that prohibited the importation of enslaved Africans.

serving as president. This act, which took effect the next year, followed the US Constitution's specification that the importation of enslaved Africans not be outlawed until 1808 at the earliest.

Even though this law marked the end of the slave trade, slavery would continue to exist in the United States until the mid-nineteenth century. During these years, men, women, and children would be trapped in the system. What was life like for them? Each individual had his or her own unique story about what it was like to be enslaved by white people in America.

SOLOMON IN HIS PLANTATION SUIT.

Solomon Northrup, born a free black man, was a talented violinist. He was kidnapped and sold into slavery, where he remained for twelve years. He wrote an autobiography about his experience.

3 Enslaved Men Tell Their Stories

There is a rich collection of writings and interviews from men and women about what it was like to live enslaved. Olaudah Equiano, whose work you read in the first chapter, is said to have written the first slave autobiography. With it, he began an important literary tradition: the slave narrative.

Slave Narratives

Historians believe that some six thousand published narratives exist today. Some of these, like that of Equiano as well as the famous works of Frederick Douglass (*Narrative of the Life of Frederick Douglass*) and Harriet Jacobs (*Incidents in the Life of a Slave Girl*), are book-length autobiographies. Historians believe there are about two hundred of these. These works became powerful tools in the abolitionists' war on slavery. How better to describe the horrors of the institution than in the words of those trapped in it?

Other narratives were transcribed from interviews with slaves or are brief accounts of slaves' lives told to reporters, who then published them in abolitionist newspapers. These often tell the stories of former slaves who, never having learned to read or write, could not write their own works. Both touching and appalling, these narratives describe the day-to-day experiences of people who lived in bondage. Many of these were recorded long after the slaves were free, even into the first decades of the twentieth century.

Solomon Northrup's *Twelve Years a Slave*

Born a free man in New York, Solomon Northrup was kidnapped and sold into slavery at age thirty-three, leaving behind a wife and three children. An accomplished violinist, Northrup had been lured to Washington, DC, on the promise of finding work as a professional musician there. Upon his arrival, he was beaten, drugged, and sent to Louisiana, where he was sold into slavery. It would be twelve years before he regained his freedom. In the following excerpt, Northrup describes a typical day on a plantation where he worked.

> The hands are required to be in the cotton field as soon as it is light in the morning, and, with the exception of ten or fifteen minutes, which is given them at noon to swallow their allowance of cold bacon, they are not permitted to be a moment idle until it is too dark to see, and when the moon is full, they often times labor till the middle of the night. They do not dare to stop even at dinner time, nor return to the quarters, however late it be, until the order to halt is given by the driver.
>
> The day's work over in the field, the baskets are ... carried to the gin-house, where the cotton is

weighed … A slave never approaches the gin-house with his basket of cotton but with fear. If it falls short in weight—if he has not performed the full task appointed him, he knows that he must suffer. And if he has exceeded it by ten or twenty pounds, in all probability his master will measure the next day's task accordingly. So, whether he has too little or too much, his approach to the gin-house is always with fear and trembling … After weighing, follow the whippings; and then the baskets are carried to the cotton house …

This done, the labor of the day is not yet ended, by any means. Each one must then attend to his respective chores. One feeds the mules, another the swine—another cuts the wood, and so forth … Finally, at a late hour, they reach the quarters, sleepy and overcome with the long day's toil. Then a fire must be kindled in the cabin, the corn ground in the small hand-mill, and supper, and dinner for the next day in the field, prepared.

—From Solomon Northrup, *Twelve Years a Slave: Narrative of Solomon Northrup* (Auburn, NY: Derby and Miller, 1853).

CONSIDER THIS

1. Why did an enslaved laborer have to be careful not to pick too much cotton?
2. What do you think it was like for Northup to have been thrust into slavery after being born a free man?

KEY TERMS AND CONCEPTS

From Solomon Northrup's *Twelve Years a Slave*:
driver A slave driver, or a person who oversees the work of enslaved laborers.
gin A cotton gin.

From Francis Henderson's account:
bedtick Mattress.
hoe cakes Thin cornmeal pancakes.
peck A unit of dry measure equal to 8 quarts.

From Richard Toler's interview:
castah oil and tu'pentine Castor oil and turpentine.
cullud Colored, a dated, now offensive term to refer to black people.
ouah Our.
pa'taculah Particular; picky.

Francis Henderson's Account of Living Conditions

Enslaved laborers were afforded the bare minimum in terms of life's necessities. Although field workers were expected to withstand backbreaking labor from dawn until well after dusk, many owners scarcely gave them enough food to sustain them. Quarters for enslaved people were often poorly made and drafty, with leaky roofs. The dirt floors turned to mud when it rained. Some people weren't given shoes, and most had no more than a few items of clothing to protect them from icy winters or the

Enslaved Africans often lived in poorly built structures with dirt floors.

blazing sun of a Southern summer. In the following passage, Francis Henderson describes what life was like on the plantation where he lived, outside Washington, DC.

> Our houses were but log huts—the tops partly open—rain would come through … everything would be dirty and muddy … My bed and bedstead consisted of a board wide enough to sleep on—one end on a stool, the other placed near the fire. My pillow consisted of my jacket—my covering was whatever I could get. My bedtick was the board itself … I only remember

having but one blanket from my owners up to the age of nineteen, when I ran away.

Our allowance was given weekly—a peck of sifted corn meal, a dozen and a half herrings, two and a half pounds of pork. Some of the boys would eat this up in three days—then they had to steal, or they could not perform their daily tasks … I do not remember one slave but who stole some things—they were driven to it as a matter of necessity. I myself did this—many a time have I, with others, run among the stumps in chase of a sheep, that we might have something to eat … In regard to cooking, sometimes many have to cook at one fire, and before all could get to the fire to bake hoe cakes, the overseer's horn would sound: then they must go at any rate. Many a time I have gone along eating a piece of bread and meat, or herring broiled on the coals—I never sat down at a table to eat except at harvest time … In harvest time, the cooking is done at the great house, as the hands they have are wanted in the field. This was more like people, and we liked it, for we sat down then at meals.

—Reprinted in Steve Mintz, ed., *African American Voices: The Life Cycle of Slavery*, 2nd ed., (Naugatuck, CT: Brandywine Press, 1999).

CONSIDER THIS

1. Why do you think that slave masters only gave enslaved laborers barely enough food or clothing to survive?

Richard Toler: "I Sho' Is Glad I Ain't No Slave No Moah"

Between 1936 and 1938, government-funded writers interviewed more than 2,300 former slaves in seventeen states. These interviews, conducted by the Federal Writers' Project during the Great Depression, offered those who were previously enslaved an opportunity to tell their stories. It was an opportunity they might not otherwise have had. The following is the narrative of Richard Toler, who had been enslaved in Virginia during the Civil War.

> Ah never had no good times till ah was free … Ah was bo'n on Mastah Tolah's plantation down in ole V'ginia … We lived in a cabin way back of the big house, me and mah pappy and mammy and two brothahs.
>
> Ah never went to school. Learned to read and write my name after ah was free in night school, but they [the masters] nevah allowed us to have a book in ouah hand, and we couldn't have no money neither. If we had money we had to tu'n it ovah to ouah ownah. Chu'ch was not allowed …
>
> We was nevah allowed no pa'ties, and when they had goin' ons at the big house, we had to clear out. Ah had to wo'k hard all the time every day in the week. Had to min' the cows and calves, and when ah got older ah had to hoe in the field … Ah've done about evahthing in mah life, blacksmith and stone mason, ca'penter, evahthing but brick-layin' …
>
> Befo' the wah we never had no good times. They took good care of us, though. As pa'taculah with slave as with the stock … And if we claimed bein' sick, they'd

give us a dose of castah oil and tu'pentine. That was the principal medicine cullud folks had to take, and sometimes salts ... And if we was real sick, they had the Doctah fo' us.

We had very bad eatin'. Bread, meat, water. And they fed it to us in a trough, jes' like the hogs. And ah went in [my] shirt till I was 16, nevah had no clothes. And the flo' in ouah cabin was dirt, and at night we'd jes' take a blanket and lay down on the flo'. The dog was supe'ior to us; they would take him in the house.

I sho' is glad I ain't no slave no moah.

—From an interview with Richard Toler. Interviewed by Ruth Thompson, no date. *WPA Slave Narrative Project, Ohio Narratives*, Vol. 12.

CONSIDER THIS

1. Despite Toler's descriptions of the terrible conditions in which he lived, he still says that his masters took good care of him. Why do you think he feels that way?
2. Why do you think he wasn't allowed to read, write, have money, or attend church?

The Marks of This Treatment

The hardships of slavery were many. There was the psychological wear and tear of white slave owners treating enslaved people as less than human and giving them no control over their lives. Additionally, slaves endured unending labor, restrictive rules and regulations, and the fear of losing one's family. Slave owners also doled out brutal physical punishment. All these factors merged to make an enslaved life one of great difficulty.

The following two accounts document the inhumane treatment of enslaved laborers at the hands of slaveholders. In the first, abolitionist and escaped slave Frederick Douglass details the variety of reasons why an enslaved person might be punished.

> A mere look, word, or motion,—a mistake, accident, or want of power,—are all matters for which a slave may be whipped at any time. Does a slave look dissatisfied? It is said, he has the devil in him, and it must be whipped out. Does he speak loudly when spoken to by his master? Then he is getting high-minded, and should be taken down a button-hole lower. Does he forget to pull off his hat at the approach of a white person? Then he is wanting in reverence, and should be whipped for it. Does he ever venture to vindicate his conduct, when censured for it? Then he is guilty of impudence,—one of the greatest crimes of which a slave can be guilty. Does he ever venture to suggest a different mode of doing things from that pointed out by his master? He is indeed presumptuous, and getting above himself.
>
> —From Frederick Douglass, *Narrative of the Life of Frederick Douglass, An American Slave*. Reprinted in Henry Louis Gates Jr., ed., *The Classic Slave Narratives* (New York: Signet Classic, 2002).

CONSIDER THIS

1. Why do you think there were so many things an enslaved person could be punished for?

This second account is an excerpt from the autobiography of Moses Roper. He describes what happened to him when he tried to escape.

> My master gave me a hearty dinner, the best he ever did give me; but it was to keep me from dying before he had given me all the flogging he intended. After dinner he took me up to the log-house, stripped me quite naked, fastened a rail up very high, tied my hands to the rail, fastened my feet together, put a rail between my feet, and stood on the end of it to hold me down; the two sons then gave me fifty lashes each, the son-in-law another fifty, and Mr. Gooch himself fifty more …
>
> After this, they took me to the blacksmith's shop, got two large bars of iron, which they bent around my feet, each bar weighing twenty pounds [9 kg], and put a heavy log-chain on my neck …
>
> After this … I stayed with him several months, and did my work very well. It was about the beginning of 1832, when he took off my irons, and being in dread of him, he having threatened me with more punishment, I attempted again to escape from him. At this time I got into North Carolina: but a reward having been offered for me, a Mr. Robinson caught me, and chained me to a chair, upon which he sat up with me all night, and next day proceeded home with me. This was Saturday. Mr. Gooch had gone to church, several miles from his house. When he came back, the first thing he did was to pour some tar upon my head, then rubbed it all over my face, took a torch with pitch on, and set it on fire; he put

Slave owners physically punished enslaved Africans for a variety of reasons, from them running away to them not being productive enough. Here, a young Abraham Lincoln (*second from left*) witnesses a whipping.

it out before it did me very great injury, but the pain which I endured was the most excruciating, nearly all my hair having been burnt off.

On Monday, he puts irons on me again, weighing nearly fifty pounds [23 kg]. He threatened me again on the Sunday with another flogging; and on the Monday morning, before daybreak, I got away again, with my irons on, and was about three hours going a distance of two miles [1.6 kilometers]. I had gone a good distance, when I met with a coloured man, who got some wedges, and took my irons off. However, I was caught again, and put into prison in Charlotte, where Mr. Gooch came, and took me back to Chester. He asked me how I got my irons off. They having been got off by a slave, I would not answer his question, for fear of getting the man punished. Upon this he put the fingers of my hands into a vice, and squeezed all the nails off. He then had my feet put on an anvil, and ordered a man to beat my toes, till he smashed some of my nails off. The marks of this treatment still remain upon me, some of my nails never having grown perfect since.

—From Moses Roper, *Narrative of the Adventures and Escape of Moses Roper* (Berwick-upon-Tweed: published for the author, and printed at the Warder Office, 1848).

KEY TERMS AND CONCEPTS

From Frederick Douglass's autobiography:

censured Blamed or punished.

impudence Boldness or disrespect.

presumptuous Doing more than what is appropriate or permitted.

reverence Respect.

vindicate To clear from blame.

From Moses Grandy's narrative:

consternation Unexpected anxiety or distress.

dram Money.

leave Permission.

From Andrew Goodman's account:

kilt Killed.

'lasses Molasses.

n***** A now very offensive term used to refer to black people.

noddin' Dozing off to sleep.

CONSIDER THIS

1. Consider how terrible the conditions of slavery must have been for Moses Roper to have risked enduring this sort of torture. What would you have done in his position?

The Last Time Moses Grandy Saw His Wife

Most slaves lived in nuclear families, or a family that consisted of a mother, a father, and children. However, these families faced a constant threat of separation. State laws did not recognize marriages between enslaved couples. Additionally, owners, not parents, held legal authority over enslaved children.

Among the numerous difficulties that slaves endured, perhaps none was so painful as the forced separation of family members—husband from wife, mother from child. A husband could be sold from his plantation to another hundreds of miles away. A mother could be put up for auction at the whim of the slave owner. A slave owner would sell an enslaved individual if he needed money or wanted to punish someone. Whatever the reason, once separated, family members were unlikely to see each other again.

In the following account, Moses Grandy describes the day his wife was sold. Grandy, born in North Carolina around 1786, escaped from slavery in 1833. With the help of the American Anti-Slavery Society, he published his autobiography in 1843.

> I married a slave belonging to Enoch Sawyer ... I left her at home ... one Thursday morning, when we had been married about eight months ... On the Friday, as I was at work as usual with the boats, I heard a noise behind me, on the road which ran by the side of the canal: I turned to look, and saw a gang of slaves coming. When they came up to me, one of them cried out, "Moses, my dear!" I wondered who among them should know me, and found it was my wife. She cried out to me, "I am gone." I was struck with consternation. Mr. Rogerson was with them, on his horse, armed with pistols. I said to him, "for God's sake, have you bought my wife?" He said he

had; when I asked him what she had done; he said she had done nothing, but that her master wanted money.

He drew out a pistol, and said that if I went near the waggon on which she was, he would shoot me. I asked for leave to shake hands with her, which he refused, but said I might stand at a distance and talk with her. My heart was so full, that I could say very little. I asked leave to give her a dram: he told Mr. Burgess, the man who was with him, to get down and carry it to her. I gave her the little money I had in my pocket, and bid her farewell. I have never seen or heard of her from that day to this. I loved her as I loved my life.

—From *Narrative of the Life of Moses Grandy; Late a Slave in the United States of America* (London: C. Gilpin, 1843).

CONSIDER THIS

1. Why do you think Mr. Rogerson wouldn't let Grandy shake hands with his wife?

Andrew Goodman's Opinion of Slavery

More often than not, the slave narratives tell difficult and complex stories. These stories are of tired, overworked, abused, and grieving individuals. These stories are about slave owners who were heartless at best and cruel or even murderous at worst.

Another kind of narrative exists, however. It offers a brief glimpse of a less brutal existence in this dark period of American history. In the following passage from Andrew Goodman of Texas, the former slave describes the kindness of his master. Despite his

Andrew Goodman was interviewed about his experiences of slavery during the Great Depression, a period of financial crisis in the United States during the 1930s.

master's kindness, however, it is important to remember that he still owned the people to whom he was being kind.

> I was born in slavery and I think them days was better for the n*****s than the days we see now. One thing was, I never was cold and hungry when my old master lived, and I has been plenty hungry and cold a lot of times since he is gone. But sometimes I think Marse Goodman was the bestest man God made in a long time ...
>
> Old Marse never 'lowed none of his n***** families separated ... He thought it right and fittin' that folks stay together, though I heard tell of some that didn't think so.
>
> My Missus was just as good as Marse Bob. My maw was a puny little woman that wasn't able to do work in the fields, and she puttered round the house for the Missus, doin' little odd jobs. I played round with little Miss Sallie and little Mr. Bob, and I ate with them and slept with them. I used to sweep off the steps and do things, and she'd brag on me. Many is the time I'd get to noddin' and go to sleep, and she'd pick me up and put me in bed with her chillen.
>
> Marse Bob didn't put his little n*****s in the fields till they's big 'nough to work ... He didn't never put the n*****s out in bad weather. He give us something to do, in out of the weather, like shellin' corn, and the women could spin and knit ...
>
> We raised cotton and grain and chickens and vegetables, and most anything anybody could ask for.

Some places the masters give out a peck of meal and so many pounds of meat to a family for them a week's rations, and if they ate it up that was all they got. But Marse Bob always give out plenty, and said, "If you need more you can have it, 'cause ain't any going to suffer on my place."

He built us a church, and a old man, Kenneth Lyons, who was a slave of the Lyons' family nearby, used to get a pass every Sunday mornin' and come preach to us. He was a man of good learnin' and the best preacher I ever heard ... Then on Sunday afternoon, Marse Bob learned us to read and write. He told us we oughta get all the learnin' we could.

Once a week the slaves could have any night they want for a dance or frolic ... Marse Bob give us chickens or kilt a fresh beef or let us make 'lasses candy. We could choose any night, 'cept in the fall of the year. Then we worked awful hard and didn't have the time ... Marse always give us from Christmas Eve through New Year's Day off, to make up for the hard work in the fall ...

Course, we used to hear about other places where they had n***** drivers and beat the slaves. But I never did see or hear tell of one of master's slaves gittin' a beatin' ... Marse Bob never had no n*****s to run off.

—Reprinted in Norman R. Yetman, ed., *Voices from Slavery: 100 Authentic Slave Narratives* (Minneola, NY: Dover, 2000).

CONSIDER THIS

1. Why do you think Goodman believes his life in slavery was better than it was after gaining his freedom?
2. List several ways that Goodman's experience was different from those of many other slaves, including those described in the narratives you have read here.

The Other Half of the Story

The thousands of narratives available to us today provide a view of slavery from many diverse perspectives. However, the voices of enslaved men are only a part of the story. Enslaved women had their own similar but also unique experiences within the system of slavery.

Although it was illegal in many places to teach enslaved people to read and write, some learned in secret. Here, one enslaved woman reads to a group of children.

4 Enslaved Women Tell Their Stories

In colonial America and through the twentieth century, few women, regardless of race, had their voices heard. The slave narratives and autobiographies of black women gave women a voice. Interviewers listened closely to these women's stories. For this reason, we have a captivating picture of what it was like to be both a woman and enslaved in nineteenth-century America.

Elizabeth Keckley's Account of a Sold Boy

Elizabeth Hobbs Keckley was born into slavery in 1818. By 1855, she had saved enough money to buy her freedom. She eventually worked at the White House as a dressmaker for Mary Todd Lincoln. At age fifty, she published her autobiography, *Behind the Scenes, or, Thirty Years a Slave and Four Years in the White House*. Portions of her autobiography are reprinted here. In this selection, Keckley recounts her childhood memory of a young boy who was separated from his family and sold.

> When I was about seven years old I witnessed, for the first time, the sale of a human being. We were living at Prince Edward, in Virginia, and master had just purchased his hogs for the winter, for which he was unable to pay in full. To escape from his embarrassment it was necessary to sell one of the slaves. Little Joe, the son of the cook, was selected as the victim. His mother was ordered to dress him up in his Sunday clothes, and send him to the house. He came in with a bright face, was placed in the scales, and was sold, like the hogs, at so much per pound. His mother was kept in ignorance of the transaction, but her suspicions were aroused. When her son started for Petersburgh in the wagon, the truth began to dawn upon her mind, and she pleaded piteously that her boy should not be taken from her; but master quieted her by telling her that he was simply going to town with the wagon, and would be back in the morning.
>
> Morning came, but little Joe did not return to his mother. Morning after morning passed, and the mother went down to the grave without ever seeing her child again. One day she was whipped for grieving for her lost boy. Colonel Burwell never liked to see one of his slaves wear a sorrowful face, and those who offended in this particular way were always punished. Alas! the sunny face of the slave is not always an indication of sunshine in the heart.

KEY TERMS AND CONCEPTS

From Elizabeth Hobbs Keckley's account of Little Joe's sale:
piteously Deserving of compassion.
transaction The buying or selling of something.

From Elizabeth Hobbs Keckley's account of her flogging:
exasperate To intensely irritate.
flog To beat with a whip.
ply To work steadily.
remiss Negligent or lacking care in one's duties.
smother To extinguish.
thunderstruck Shocked.

—From Elizabeth Keckley, *Behind the Scenes, or, Thirty Years a Slave and Four Years in the White House*. Schomburg Library of Nineteenth-Century Black Women Writers (New York: Oxford University Press, 1989).

CONSIDER THIS

1. Why didn't the master tell Little Joe's mother what he planned to do? Why do you think she was suspicious?

Elizabeth Keckley's Account of Her Flogging

Cruel punishment was not reserved solely for male slaves. Women, too, faced the lash and other harsh forms of punishment. In the following passage, Keckley recalls being whipped by her master's friend, at whose home she had been working.

> Mr. Bingham came to the door and asked me to go with him to his study. Wondering what he meant by his strange request, I followed him, and when we had entered the study he closed the door, and in his blunt way remarked: "Lizzie, I am going to flog you." I was thunderstruck, and tried to think if I had been remiss in anything. I could not recollect of doing anything to deserve punishment, and with surprise exclaimed: "Whip me, Mr. Bingham! what for?"
>
> "No matter," he replied, "I am going to whip you, so take down your dress this instant."
>
> Recollect, I was eighteen years of age, was a woman fully developed, and yet this man coolly bade me take down my dress. I drew myself up proudly, firmly, and said: "No, Mr. Bingham, I shall not take down my dress before you. Moreover, you shall not whip me unless you prove the stronger. Nobody has a right to whip me but my own master, and nobody shall do so if I can prevent it."
>
> My words seemed to exasperate him. He seized a rope, caught me roughly, and tried to tie me. I resisted with all my strength, but he was the stronger of the two, and after a hard struggle succeeded in binding my hands and tearing my dress from my back. Then he picked up

a rawhide, and began to ply it freely over my shoulders. With steady hand and practised eye he would raise the instrument of torture, nerve himself for a blow, and with fearful force the rawhide descended upon the quivering flesh. It cut the skin, raised great welts, and the warm blood trickled down my back. Oh God! I can feel the torture now—the terrible, excruciating agony of those moments. I did not scream; I was too proud to let my tormentor know what I was suffering ...

As soon as I was released, stunned with pain, bruised and bleeding, I went home and rushed into the presence of the pastor and his wife [her master and mistress], wildly exclaiming: "Master Robert, why did you let Mr. Bingham flog me? What have I done that I should be so punished?"

"Go away," he gruffly answered, "do not bother me."

I would not be put off thus. "What have I done? I will know why I have been flogged."

I saw his cheeks flush with anger, but I did not move. He rose to his feet, and on my refusing to go without an explanation, seized a chair, struck me, and felled me to the floor. I rose, bewildered, almost dead with pain, crept to my room, dressed my bruised arms and back as best I could, and then lay down, but not to sleep. No, I could not sleep, for I was suffering mental as well as bodily torture. My spirit rebelled against the unjustness that had been inflicted upon me, and though I tried to smother my anger and to forgive those who had been so cruel to me, it was impossible. It seems that Mr. Bingham had pledged himself to

Mrs. Burwell [Keckley's mistress] to subdue what he called my "stubborn pride."

—From Elizabeth Keckley, *Behind the Scenes, or, Thirty Years a Slave and Four Years in the White House*. Schomburg Library of Nineteenth-Century Black Women Writers (New York: Oxford University Press, 1989).

CONSIDER THIS

1. The physical pain of this punishment was terrible, but what other aspects of Keckley's experience made the situation even worse?
2. What was Keckley's master's occupation? Should this have had some effect on his treatment of her?

Harriet Jacobs's *Incidents in the Life of a Slave Girl*

"I was so fondly shielded," Harriet Jacobs wrote of her childhood. "I never dreamed I was a piece of merchandise." Jacobs lived in a house with her brother and parents, both of whom were children of white fathers and black mothers. When her mother died, six-year-old Harriet learned "by the talk around me, that I was a slave."

In the following passage, she describes turning fifteen years old. She was a beautiful girl. Her master, who was forty years older, began to take a sexual interest in her. Harriet took strong measures to avoid his pursuit, but he made her life extremely difficult. Unfortunately, what Harriet describes was all too common an experience for enslaved women.

I now entered on my fifteenth year—a sad epoch in the life of a slave girl. My master began to whisper

Incidents in the Life of a Slave Girl explores Harriet Jacobs's experience as a young enslaved woman and mother of two. In it, she details her escape from slavery and her attempts to secure freedom for herself and her children.

foul words in my ear. Young as I was, I could not remain ignorant of their import ... He peopled my young mind with unclean images, such as only a vile monster could think of. I turned from him with disgust and hatred. But he was my master. I was compelled to live under the same roof with him ... He told me I was his property; that I must be subject to his will in all things. My soul revolted against the mean tyranny. But where could I turn for protection? ...

[In the life of a slave girl] there is no shadow of law to protect her from insult, from violence, or even from death; all these are inflicted by fiends who bear the shape of men. The mistress, who ought to protect the helpless victim, has no other feelings towards her but those of jealousy and rage ...

Even the little child, who is accustomed to wait on her mistress and her children, will learn, before she is twelve years old, why it is that her mistress hates such and such a one among the slaves ... She listens to violent outbreaks of jealous passion, and cannot help understanding what is the cause. She will become prematurely knowing in evil things. Soon she will learn to tremble when she hears her master's footfall. She will be compelled to realize that she is no longer a child. If God has bestowed beauty upon her, it will prove her greatest curse. That which commands admiration in the white woman only hastens the degradation of the female slave ...

I longed for some one to confide in ... But Dr. Flint [Jacobs's master] swore he would kill me, if I was not

KEY TERMS AND CONCEPTS

From Harriet Jacobs's narrative:

bestow To give.

degradation The condition of being defiled or degraded, or treated without respect.

epoch A time period in a person's life.

fiend An evil or cruel person, like a devil. Also, a person who is addicted to something.

footfall Footsteps.

hasten To hurry along.

import Meaning.

prematurely Ahead of the appropriate time.

tyranny Cruel or oppressive control.

From Tempe Herndon Durham's account of her marriage:

'genial Friendly.

kaze Because.

shoat A young hog.

skeered Scared.

surrender A reference to the end of the Civil War.

'twell Till.

as silent as the grave. Then, although my grandmother was all in all to me, I feared her as well as loved her ... I was very young, and felt shamefaced about telling her such impure things ...

—From Harriet Jacobs, *Incidents in the Life of a Slave Girl*. Reprinted in Henry Louis Gates Jr., *The Classic Slave Narratives* (New York: Signet Classic, 2002).

CONSIDER THIS

1. Jacobs offers explanations for why she could not tell anyone about what was happening to her. What are they?
2. According to Jacobs, who might be expected to protect a slave girl from a master's sexual advances? Why wouldn't this person help her?
3. In your own words, explain the following sentence: "That which commands admiration in the white woman only hastens the degradation of the female slave."

Religion Provides a Little Peace for Charlotte Brooks

For many enslaved Africans, religion provided a refuge, or a safe place. In the colonial years, new arrivals from Africa often continued to practice the religions of their homeland. As time passed, generations born in the New World were increasingly drawn to the faith practiced all around them: Christianity. Sometimes they went to their masters' churches, sitting in a special area reserved for people who were enslaved. Other times a preacher visited slave quarters. Often, though, people who were enslaved received little religious instruction beyond warnings to obey their masters.

Perhaps most important to enslaved Africans were the communities of faith that grew and flourished within their own world, with their friends and families. In their quarters, slaves held secret prayer meetings, some risking severe punishment for doing so. There they listened to black preachers, who often took great risks themselves by sneaking out of their plantations to spread the word of God. The following is an account from one woman about the importance of religion in her life.

> I finally got religion, and it was Aunt Jane's praying and singing them old Virginia hymns that helped me so much. Aunt Jane's marster would let her come to see me sometimes, but not often. Sometimes she would slip away from her place at night and come to see me anyhow. She would hold prayer-meeting in my house whenever she would come to see me ...
>
> If old marster heard us singing and praying he would come out and make us stop. One time, I remember, we all were having a prayer-meeting in my cabin, and marster came up to the door and hollered out, "You, Charlotte, what's all that fuss in there?" We all had to hush up for that night. I was so afraid old marster would see Aunt Jane. I knew Aunt Jane would have to suffer if her white people knew she was off at night. Marster used to say God was tired of us all hollering to him at night ...
>
> None of us listened to him about singing and praying. I tell you we used to have some good times together praying and singing. He did not want us to pray,

> but we would have our little prayer-meeting anyhow. Sometimes when we met to hold our meetings we would put a big wash-tub full of water in the middle of the floor to catch the sound of our voices when we sung. When we all sung we would march around and shake each other's hands, and we would sing easy and low, so marster could not hear us. O, how happy I used to be in those meetings, although I was a slave!
>
> —From Octavia V. Rogers, *The House of Bondage, or, Charlotte Brooks and Other Slaves, Original and Life Like* (New York: Hunt & Eaton, 1890).

CONSIDER THIS

1. Why do you think masters tried to prevent slaves from meeting?
2. Why do you think religion may have been important to those who were enslaved?

Tempe Herndon Durham's Wedding

If religion provided one source of comfort, family provided another. Enslaved people could not legally marry, but this did not keep them from holding wedding ceremonies. It certainly did not prevent them from forming strong lifelong unions, as Moses Grandy's earlier account suggests. If they were lucky, unlike Grandy, they might not be separated. However, many husbands and wives were unable to live together. Against these odds, couples built bonds that would offer them peace and comfort. Sometimes these bonds were supported by their owners.

Tempe Herndon Durham grew up on a large plantation in North Carolina, owned by George and Betsy Herndon. Tempe married Exter Durham on the front porch of the Herndons' home.

During weddings, many enslaved couples jumped over a broom. It's a custom that some African Americans still practice in the twenty-first century.

The Herndons held a lively celebration in the couple's honor. In the following narrative, she describes the happy day.

> We had a big weddin'. We was married on de front po'ch of de big house. Marse George killed a shoat an' Mis' Betsy had Georgianna, de cook, to bake a big weddin' cake all iced up white as snow wid a bride an' groom standin' in de middle holdin' han's. De table was set out in de yard under de trees, an' you ain't never seed de like of eats. All de n*****s come to de feas' ... Dat was some weddin'. I had on a white dress, white shoes an' long white gloves dat come to my elbow, an' Mis' Betsy done made me a weddin' veil out of a white net window curtain.

When she played de weddin' ma'ch on de piano, me an' Exter ma'ched down de walk an' up on de po'ch to de altar Mis' Betsy done fixed. Dat de pretties' altar I ever seed. Back 'gainst de rose vine dat was full of red roses, Mis' Betsy done put tables filled wid flowers an' white candles ... Exter done made me a weddin' ring. He made it out of a big red button wid his pocket knife. He done cut it so roun' an' polished it so smooth dat it looked like a red satin ribbon tide 'roun' my finger. Dat sho was a pretty ring. I wore it 'bout fifty years, den it got so thin dat I lost it one day in de wash tub when I was washin' clothes.

Uncle Edmond Kirby married us. He was de n***** preacher dat preached at de plantation church. After Uncle Edmond said de las' words over me an' Exter, Marse George got to have his little fun: He say, "Come on, Exter, you an' Tempie got to jump over de broom stick backwards; you got to do dat to see which one gwine be boss of your househol'." Everybody come stan' 'roun to watch. Marse George hold de broom 'bout a foot high off de floor. De one dat jump over it backwards an' never touch de handle, gwine boss de house, an' if bof of dem jump over widout touchin' it, [there won't] be no bossin', dey jus' ... be 'genial. I jumped fus', an' you ought to seed me. I sailed right over dat broom stick same as a cricket, but when Exter jump ... his feets was so big an' clumsy dat dey got all tangled up in dat broom an' he fell head long. Marse George he laugh an' laugh, an' tole Exter he [was going to] be bossed 'twell he skeered to speak less'n I tole him to speak. After de weddin' we went down to de cabin Mis' Betsy done all dressed up, but Exter couldn' stay no longer den dat night kaze he

> belonged to Marse Snipes Durham an' he had to go back home. He lef' de nex day for his plantation, but he come back every Saturday night an' stay 'twell Sunday night. We had eleven chillun. Nine was bawn befo' surrender an' two after we was set free. So I had two chillun dat wuzn' bawn in bondage. I was worth a heap to Marse George kaze I had so many chillun. De more chillun a slave had de more dey was worth. Lucy Carter was de only n***** on de plantation dat had more chillun den I had. She had twelve, but her chillun was sickly an' mine was muley strong an' healthy. Dey never was sick.
>
> —From "The Narrative of Tempe Herndon Durham," *Federal Writers' Project: Slave Narrative Project, Vol. 11, North Carolina, Part 1, Adams–Hunter* (1936).

CONSIDER THIS

1. Durham describes a wedding tradition known as "jumping the broom." From what she said, what is the significance of this activity?
2. Why do you think the Herndons allowed Tempe to marry Exter? What impression do you have of the Herndons after reading her description of them?
3. Durham says she was "worth a heap" to George Herndon. What does she mean by this?

Not Enough

Despite the comforts of family and religion, slavery was still slavery. Most enslaved Africans did not have the experiences that Andrew Goodman or Tempe Herndon Durham had. Many faced brutal conditions and unfair treatment. Many were desperate to be free.

The Underground Railroad, a system of people and safe houses, helped individuals escape slavery. These people risked capture by slave hunters, re-enslavement, and punishment for running away.

5 Routes to Freedom

There were many different ways that enslaved Africans tried to escape the bonds of slavery. Some attempted to revolt, or rebel, hoping to rally a sufficient force of rebels to overwhelm their masters. But these relatively rare attempts often failed. Others chose to fight smaller battles instead. Some resisted by pretending to be sick or to misunderstand instructions. Others resorted to theft, setting fires, or even murder.

The Journey to Freedom

The majority of those who fought against slavery did so by attempting escape. No one knows for sure how many enslaved Africans actually managed to reach freedom. It is estimated that anywhere between forty thousand and one hundred thousand black people escaped the confines of slavery. Meanwhile, some enslaved Africans did not run away permanently but left to visit family or to avoid sale or punishment. Sometimes groups ran away together to protest excessive work or mistreatment.

Before the Civil War, abolitionists and Northerners sympathetic to the struggle of those who were enslaved worked to build a secret network to assist runaway slaves, the Underground Railroad. It was led by courageous abolitionists such as Harriet Tubman and Levi Coffin. The Underground Railroad, neither underground nor a railroad, was a series of routes through fourteen Northern states and Canada. The secret system, which used railway terms to describe its stops (stations) and navigators (conductors), helped some men and women reach freedom in the North. However, most runaways had only themselves to rely on. Some fled to freedom using forged or borrowed documents to "document" their freedom. Others stowed away on boats or trains. A few escapees created disguises for themselves.

Failed Attempts

For many people, however, reaching Northern cities was impossible. Instead, they hid in Southern cities and swamps. Some concealed themselves in forests near their owners' homes until they were captured or until they had no choice but to return on their own.

For every successful escape, many more failed. Slave owners often reserved the most brutal treatment for people who ran away. "Nothing seems to give the slaveholders so much pleasure as the catching and torturing of fugitives," recalled William Craft, whose story is included in this chapter. Slave owners often employed the professional services of slave hunters to track down and capture people who ran away. "The slaveholders and their hired ruffians," or violent people, recalled Craft, "appear to take more pleasure in this inhuman pursuit than English sportsmen do in chasing a fox or a stag."

The Confessions of Nat Turner: The Story of a Slave Rebellion

Nat Turner led the largest and most devastating slave revolt in US history. Turner was born into slavery in Southampton County, Virginia, in 1800. He shared a hatred of slavery with his mother, who was born somewhere in Africa. As he grew up, one of his master's sons taught him to read. Soon, Turner found himself invested in religion.

After being sold, he began to feel as though he was called not only to spread the word of God but to lead people out of bondage.

This image depicts Nat Turner discussing an uprising with other enslaved men in 1831.

Others who were enslaved were drawn to his religious fervor, or passion. They began to see him as a prophet and were willing to follow him into rebellion.

The revolt began on August 22, 1831, when Turner and four other slaves attacked Turner's owners, killing everyone in the household, including an infant. In the following days, the group moved from house to house, killing any white person it encountered. At each house, more enslaved people joined Turner's cause. In two days, the rebellion led to the deaths of nearly sixty white people. Although only about seventy-five black people joined Turner's cause, authorities killed many more innocent enslaved Africans in the chaos that followed the rebellion.

Turner initially escaped capture and stayed in hiding for nearly two months. However, he was finally caught and tried for his crimes. When he was taken in, he told his story to an attorney, Thomas Gray. The attorney would publish Turner's account as *The Confessions of Nat Turner*. Officials hanged Turner less than two weeks later.

> 'Twas my object to carry terror and devastation wherever we went … I sometimes got in sight in time to see the work of death completed, viewed the mangled bodies as they lay, in silent satisfaction, and immediately started in quest of other victims—Having murdered Mrs. Waller and ten children, we started for Mr. William Williams'—having killed him and two little boys that were there; while engaged in this, Mrs. Williams fled and got some distance from the house, but she was pursued, overtaken, and compelled to get up behind one of the company, who brought her back, and after showing her the mangled

body of her lifeless husband, she was told to get down and lay by his side, where she was shot dead ...

Our number amounted now to fifty or sixty, all mounted and armed with guns, axes, swords, and clubs ... We were met by a party of white men, who had pursued our blood-stained track ... The white men, eighteen in number, approached us in about one hundred yards, when one of them fired ... I then ordered my men to fire and rush them; the few remaining stood their ground until we approached within fifty yards, when they fired and retreated ... As I saw them reloading their guns, and more coming up than I saw at first, and several of my bravest men being wounded, the others became panick struck and squandered over the field; the white men pursued and fired on us several times ...

—From *The Confessions of Nat Turner, the Leader of the Late Insurrection in Southhampton, VA* (Baltimore: Lucas & Deaver, 1831).

CONSIDER THIS

1. Did Turner appear to show any regret in his confession? Do you think his actions were justified?
2. Turner believed that God had told him to rebel. Can you think of other cases in which people have used religion to defend their actions?

KEY TERMS AND CONCEPTS

From *The Confessions of Nat Turner*:

mangled Disfigured.

squander To scatter.

From Cyrus Branch's account:

commission Responsibility or duty.

eternal salvation The Christian belief that Jesus Christ died for everyone's sins, so everyone will be rescued from sin and its consequences in the afterlife.

exhort To urge or encourage.

From the *Louisville Courier* article:

antidote A remedy to counteract poison.

arsenic A poisonous chemical.

commence To start.

deceive To trick.

plausibility Believability.

precocious Describing a child who is particularly smart for his or her age.

proprietor The owner of a business.

yellow man Perhaps meaning a man of mixed ancestry.

The Punishment of a Preacher

Shortly after the Turner rebellion, the Virginia state government enacted laws to try to prevent a similar event from happening again. In the following passage, a former slave named Cyrus Branch explains the effects of these laws. Vermont writer Elizabeth Merwin Wickham interviewed Branch when he was reunited with his family following decades of separation. His story, including this excerpt, was published in the *Manchester Journal*, a Vermont newspaper, in January 1869.

> The State Government soon after [the Turner rebellion] enacted a law prohibiting colored men entirely from preaching and exhorting, or even gathering for prayer meetings, except at the leaves of their respective owners. These were hard laws to submit to, their situation as slaves being made bearable to some only by the soothing counsels and influence of their christian brethren. But the moral courage of a few of the preachers rose superior to the laws of the land, when they were in violation of the laws of God as revealed in the Scriptures. Among such men was one Pleasant Randall, the property of Mr. Harrison, of Charles City, who deemed his commission to make the Gospel known to sinners, to be from the Lord, and not from man.
>
> When gone into Prince George County, one Saturday, to preach for a couple of days, the planters in the vicinity visited his master, Mr. Harrison, urging him to restrain Randall, or shut him up, saying, that his preaching so affected their people that they would bear beating and beating, and then hear him again at the first opportunity—they could not thus spare

their time, and the man ought, by the laws, to be hung—and they should do something to stop him, if he did not. Mr. Harrison was personally attached to the good man, and told them, that no mob should touch him; they must proceed according to law if they meant to hinder his preaching. So Randall was arrested, imprisoned, and tried, and convicted, and condemned to be hung, for making eternal salvation known to his fellows, and an early day was fixed for his execution.

—From E. M. W. (Elizabeth Merwin Wickham), "A Lost Family Found; An Authentic Narrative of Cyrus Branch and His Family, Alias John White of Manchester, Vermont," (*Manchester Journal*, January 1869).

CONSIDER THIS

1. Pleasant Randall was clearly a magnetic preacher if the people would bear beating after beating in order to listen to him. According to Cyrus Branch, Randall's main concern was for the salvation of enslaved souls. Why, then, would the planters want him stopped?
2. Think about what the First Amendment—part of the Bill of Rights—says about freedom of religion. Was it acceptable to arrest, try, and sentence Pleasant Randall to death for practicing religion?

An Enslaved Girl Poisons Her Owners

In the following newspaper account, a reporter describes the case of a family poisoned by an enslaved girl.

> A Family Poisoned by a Slave Child only Twelve Years Old. From the *Louisville Courier*, July 13.
>
> Great excitement was created yesterday by the report that poison had been administered to the family of Mrs. Patrick H. Pope ... The persons affected were Mrs. Pope, her daughter Ella, Miss Green, of Danville, Ky., and a negro servant. The poison was arsenic, which was put into the coffee-pot while it was on the table, as confessed by the slave girl, Charity, who is ten or twelve years of age. Those of the family we name, shortly after breakfast were affected with vomiting, thirst, and other indications that they had swallowed poison. Antidotes were promptly administered, and last evening, we are happy to say, all were out of danger ...
>
> The poison was obtained from the drug store of W. H. Young ... The girl Charity, in the absence of the proprietor, early in the morning applied to the attendant, a boy of 14 years, for arsenic, and said her mistress wanted to kill rats. The boy refused, saying Mr. Young had given strict orders to let no servant or minor have arsenic without an order. He told her to get it from her mistress. She went out, and in a

few minutes returned, saying her mistress said she hadn't time to write it then, but to send it. As the lady often got articles, and deceived by the plausibility of the precocious girl, he gave the arsenic. This, as mentioned, she confesses to placing in the coffee.

Here is the story of the girl as related to Policeman Carter Tiller, who arrested her: "I told a yellow man, named Jerry, that I had been mistreated by the family, he said poison them ... He intended to do the same thing when his mistress' family came home; he told me to put it in the coffee pot, and that would kill them. I put it in before they came to breakfast; he said as soon as I saw them crying and vomiting I must run away. As soon as they commenced vomiting I went to the back gate and took to my heels and ran away. I don't know where I was going."

Tiller caught her a mile from the city.

—From the *Louisville Courier* (1858). Reprinted in the *New York Times* (July 20, 1858).

CONSIDER THIS

1. Why do you think Charity didn't know where to go?

Henry "Box" Brown: Shipped to Freedom

Although Henry Brown would later describe his life in slavery as "tolerable," one event drove him to attempt escape: the sale of his wife and three children. Knowing the dangers he faced if he ran away, Brown came up with a clever plan.

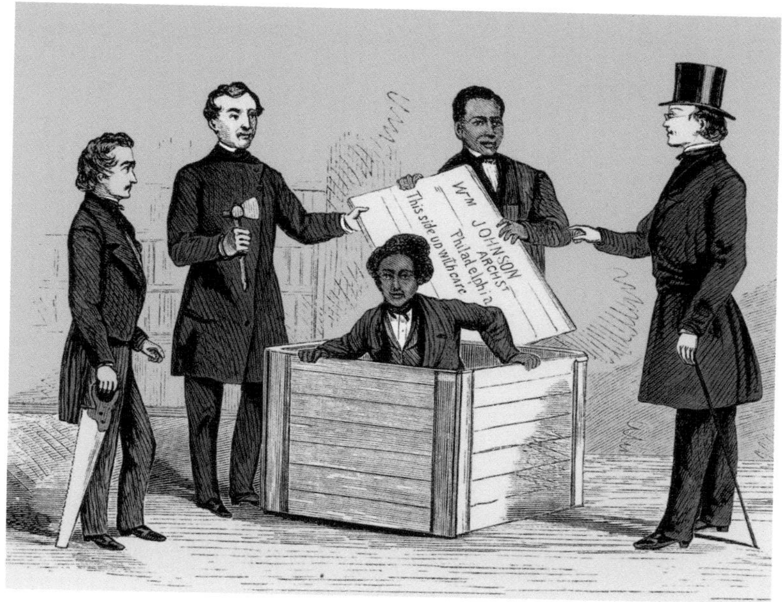

Henry "Box" Brown escaped to Philadelphia, Pennsylvania, in a box in 1849 with the aid of a shopkeeper and several abolitionists.

William Still of Philadelphia wrote the following account of Brown's story. Still, a freeborn black man, helped many black people find their way to freedom. He wrote the first detailed record of the Underground Railroad, of which Brown's story is a part. Still's work remains an important contribution to the study of slavery.

> Brown counted well the cost before venturing upon his hazardous undertaking. Ordinary modes of travel he concluded might prove disastrous to his hopes; he, therefore, hit upon a new invention altogether, which was to have himself boxed up and forwarded to Philadelphia direct by express. The size of the box and how it was to be made to fit him most comfortably, was of his own ordering. Two feet eight inches

[81 centimeters] deep, two feet [61 cm] wide, and three feet [91 cm] long were the exact dimensions of the box, lined with baize. His resources in regard to food and water consisted of the following: One bladder of water and a few small biscuits. His mechanical implement to meet the death-struggle for fresh air, all told, was one large gimlet. Satisfied that it would be far better to peril his life for freedom in this way than to remain under the galling yoke of Slavery, he entered his box, which was safely nailed up and hooped with five hickory hoops, and then was addressed by his … friend, James A. Smith, a shoe dealer, to Wm. H. Johnson, Arch Street, Philadelphia, marked, "This side up with care." … It was twenty-six hours from the time he left Richmond until his arrival in the city of Brotherly Love. The notice, "This side up, etc.," did not avail with the different expressmen, who hesitated not to handle the box in the usual rough manner … For a while they actually had the box upside down, and had him on his head for miles.

[Brown arrives at his destination.]

The witnesses will never forget that moment. Saw and hatchet quickly had the five hickory hoops cut and the lid off, and the marvelous resurrection of Brown ensued. Rising up in the box, he reached out his hand, saying, "How do you do, gentlemen?" The little assemblage hardly knew what to think or do at the moment.

—From William Still, *Still's Underground Railroad Records*, rev. ed. (Philadelphia: William Still, 1883).

KEY TERMS AND CONCEPTS

From William Still's account of Henry Brown's escape:

baize A coarse fabric.

bladder A container.

galling Humiliating or irritating.

gimlet A tool to drill holes.

implement A tool.

peril Risk.

resurrection Rebirth.

yoke An oppressive restraint usually used on animals.

From William Craft's account:

consent Permission.

countenance Face.

fancy To believe or think.

invalid A weak or disabled person.

perseverance Persistence.

poultice A warm, often medicated dressing for a wound.

propriety Decency or politeness.

CONSIDER THIS

1. Measure out the dimension of the box in which Henry Brown traveled: "two feet eight inches deep, two feet wide, and three feet long." Now try lying in a position where you fit in that box for ten minutes. Do you think you could have lasted twenty-six hours?

Ellen and William Craft: A Smart Plan

In December 1848, William and Ellen Craft, husband and wife, developed a brilliant plan of escape. It was one that would allow them to take public transportation out of Georgia, all the way to Philadelphia, staying in fine hotels along the way. It worked, and they made their way to Boston. Unfortunately, their masters eventually discovered where they were and sent slave hunters to bring them back.

The Crafts were determined not to return to a life of bondage. With the help of abolitionists, they moved to England, where slavery was illegal. After the Civil War, the couple returned to the United States. They bought a farm and opened a school for black children. The following is William's account of their extraordinary plan.

> Knowing that slaveholders have the privilege of taking their slaves to any part of the country they think proper, it occurred to me that, as my wife was nearly white, I might get her to disguise herself as an invalid gentleman, and assume to be my master, while I could attend as his slave, and that in this manner we might effect our escape …
>
> I went to different parts of the town, at odd times, and purchased things piece by piece … and took them home to the house where my wife resided … When we fancied we had everything ready the time was fixed for the flight. But we knew it would not do to start off without first getting our masters' consent to be away for a few days. Had we left without this, they would soon have had us back into slavery, and probably we should never have got another fair opportunity of even attempting to escape.

Some of the best slaveholders will sometimes give their favourite slaves a few days' holiday at Christmas time; so, after no little amount of perseverance on my wife's part, she obtained a pass from her mistress, allowing her to be away for a few days. The cabinet-maker with whom I worked gave me a similar paper …

When the thought flashed across my wife's mind, that it was customary for travellers to register their names in the visitors' book at hotels, as well as in the clearance or Custom-house book at Charleston, South Carolina—it made our spirits droop within us.

So, while sitting in our little room upon the verge of despair, all at once my wife raised her head, and with a smile upon her face, which was a moment before bathed in tears, said, "I think I have it! … I think I can make a poultice and bind up my right hand in a sling, and with propriety ask the officers to register my name for me … "

It then occurred to her that the smoothness of her face might betray her; so she decided to make another poultice, and put it in a white handkerchief to be worn under the chin, up the cheeks, and to tie over the head. This nearly hid the expression of the countenance, as well as the beardless chin …

We sat up all night discussing the plan, and making preparations. Just before the time arrived, in the morning, for us to leave, I cut off my wife's hair square at the back of the head, and got her to dress in the disguise and stand out on the floor. I found that she made a most respectable looking gentleman.

—From William Craft, *Running a Thousand Miles for Freedom* (London: William Twedie, 1860).

CONSIDER THIS

1. Briefly describe the Crafts' plan for escape. What characteristic of Ellen's made it possible?
2. Why were the Crafts worried about the fact that travelers had to register their names at hotels and the customhouse?
3. Why do you think the Crafts did not try to escape with Ellen acting as a white woman?

Help from White Allies

Enslaved people worked hard to fight against the system that oppressed them through revolts and escapes. However, they were not the only people working for their freedom. There were also white people who opposed slavery, known as abolitionists. They hoped to end the terrible institution. They made their arguments in public forums such as newspapers and pleaded to governing bodies like Congress. Ultimately, it became clear that perhaps a fight, on a much bigger scale than Nat Turner's rebellion, would be necessary to end slavery in the United States.

Ellen Craft could pass for a white person. She traveled with her husband as her attendant from Georgia to Massachusetts to escape slavery. Her husband wrote an account of their daring adventure.

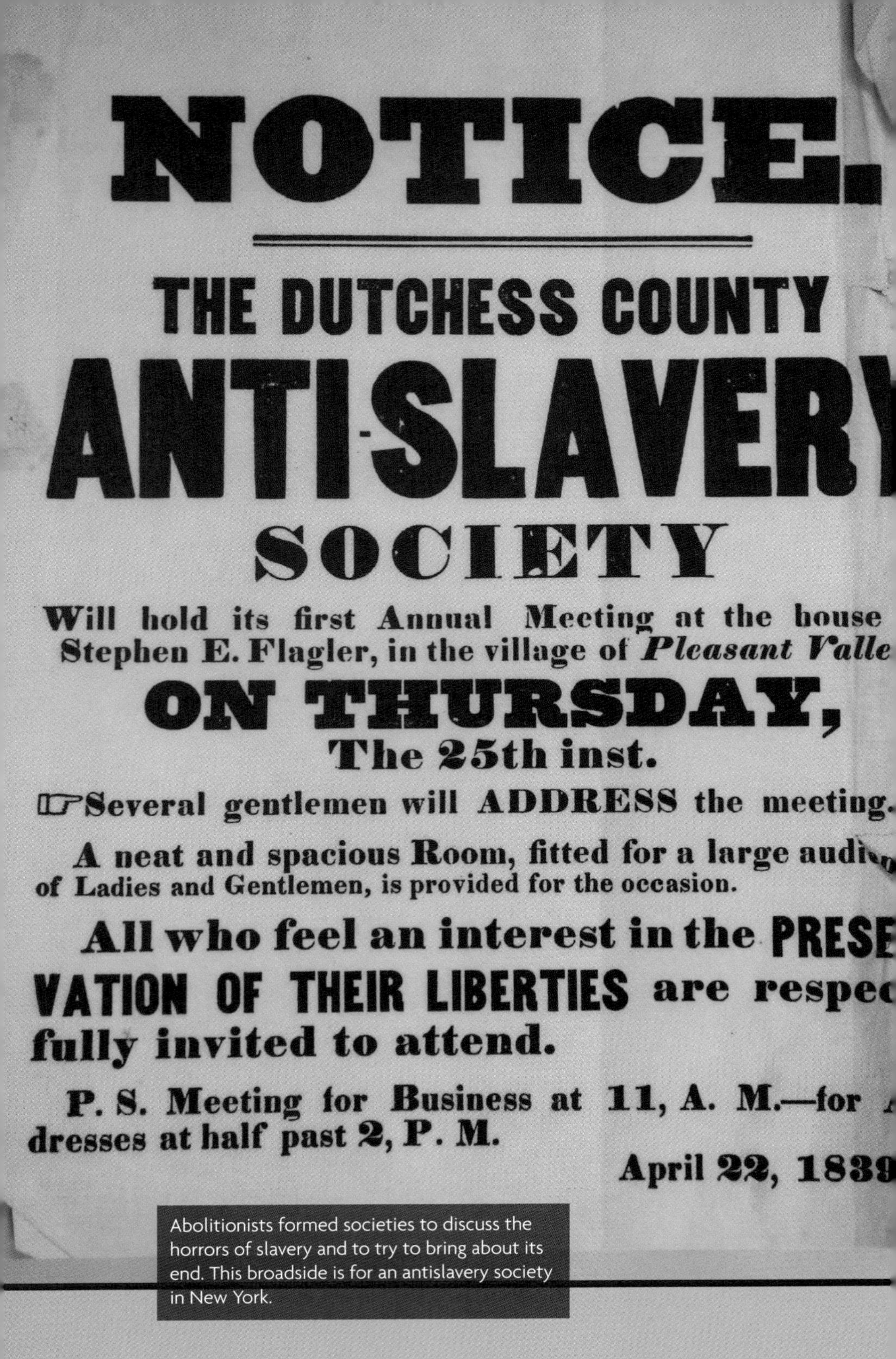

NOTICE.

THE DUTCHESS COUNTY ANTI-SLAVERY SOCIETY

Will hold its first Annual Meeting at the house
Stephen E. Flagler, in the village of *Pleasant Valle*

ON THURSDAY,

The 25th inst.

☞Several gentlemen will ADDRESS the meeting.

A neat and spacious Room, fitted for a large audi
of Ladies and Gentlemen, is provided for the occasion.

All who feel an interest in the PRESE VATION OF THEIR LIBERTIES are respec fully invited to attend.

P. S. Meeting for Business at 11, A. M.—for
dresses at half past 2, P. M.

April 22, 1839

Abolitionists formed societies to discuss the horrors of slavery and to try to bring about its end. This broadside is for an antislavery society in New York.

6

The Abolitionists' Effort

In the half century leading up to the Civil War, conflict intensified between people who supported slavery and people who were against it. By the 1830s, abolitionists started to gain political power. As that happened, the nation's future grew ever more uncertain. The desire to end slavery no longer came from a tiny minority. In this tense atmosphere, conversations surrounding slavery found their way to the very center of political power.

Congress Intervenes

In an attempt to calm both sides, Congress passed a series of laws known as the Compromise of 1850. The compromise gave proslavery and antislavery individuals some of what they wanted. One law meant to calm abolitionists ensured that slavery would be prohibited in California, for example. Meanwhile, the Fugitive Slave Act was intended to satisfy the slave owners. According to this law, a person suspected of being a runaway could be arrested and turned over to anyone who claimed to own him or her—with nothing more than the person's sworn word of ownership. Suspected runaways did not have the right to a trial by jury, nor could they testify on their own behalf. Any person who helped an enslaved person escape by providing shelter, food, or any other form of assistance could be punished by six months in prison and a $1,000 fine. Since slave hunters received a reward, the act also encouraged some to kidnap free black people and sell them to slave owners.

Ironically, the results of the Fugitive Slave Act would be exactly the opposite of what its framers intended. Abolitionists despised the new law. In fact, rather than discouraging them from helping black people escape slavery, the law drove their efforts and helped push the country closer to civil war.

William Lloyd Garrison and the *Liberator*

Many early abolitionists believed the process of emancipation should be gradual. As time went on, this attitude changed, in part because of the work of William Lloyd Garrison, a writer, editor, and abolitionist. An outspoken critic of slavery, Garrison started an antislavery paper, the *Liberator*, in 1831.

For thirty-five years, the paper attacked not only slaveholders but also those abolitionists who were opposed to rapid change. Some people considered Garrison's position too radical, but it opened the eyes of many. The following is a portion of his editorial "To the Public," published in the first issue of the *Liberator*.

> I shall strenuously contend for the immediate enfranchisement of our slave population. [O]n the Fourth of July, 1829, in an address on slavery, I unreflectingly assented to the popular but pernicious doctrine of gradual abolition. I seize this opportunity

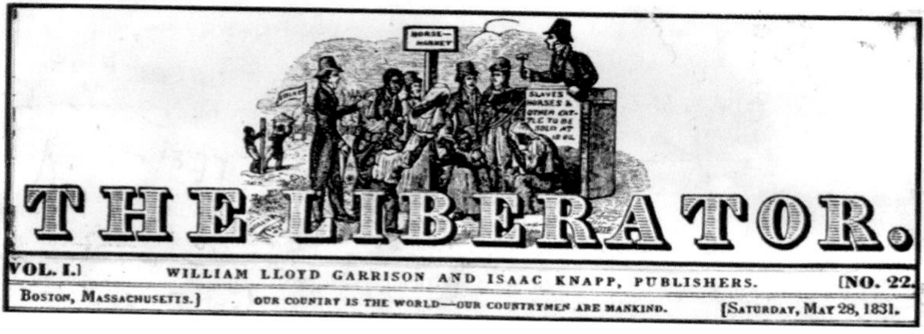
THE LIBERATOR.

VOL. I.] WILLIAM LLOYD GARRISON AND ISAAC KNAPP, PUBLISHERS. [NO. 22.

BOSTON, MASSACHUSETTS.] OUR COUNTRY IS THE WORLD—OUR COUNTRYMEN ARE MANKIND. [SATURDAY, MAY 28, 1831.

William Lloyd Garrison's Boston-based paper the *Liberator* was published from 1831 to 1865, the year that slavery was abolished in the United States.

to make a full and unequivocal recantation, and thus publicly to ask pardon of my God, of my country, and of my brethren the poor slaves, for having uttered a sentiment so full of timidity, injustice and absurdity …

I am aware, that many object to the severity of my language; but is there not cause for severity? I will be as harsh as truth, and as uncompromising as justice. On this subject, I do not wish to think, or speak, or write, with moderation. No! no! Tell a man whose house is on fire, to give a moderate alarm; … tell the mother to gradually extricate her babe from the fire into which it has fallen;—but urge me not to use moderation in a cause like the present. I am in earnest—I will not equivocate—I will not excuse—I will not retreat a single inch—AND I WILL BE HEARD.

—From William Lloyd Garrison, "To the Public." In *Liberator*, January 1, 1831. Reprinted in Wendell Phillips Garrison, *William Lloyd Garrison, 1805–1879: The Story of His Life, Told by His Children*, Vol. 1 (New York: The Century Company, 1885).

KEY TERMS AND CONCEPTS

From William Lloyd Garrison's "To the Public":

assent To agree.

contend To struggle or fight.

doctrine A policy.

enfranchisement Liberation from slavery.

equivocate To be indirect, or to avoid committing to a decision.

extricate To remove or free.

pardon Forgiveness.

pernicious Harmful.

recantation A retraction, or the action of taking back a former statement.

strenuously With great effort.

unequivocal Without a doubt.

From Angelina Grimké's *Appeal to the Christian Women of the South*:

abject Without pride or dignity.

ameliorate To ease.

corporal chastisement Physical punishment.

discountenance To disapprove of.

induce To persuade.

propagate To spread.

CONSIDER THIS

1. How do you think the metaphor about a baby in a fire helped Garrison to persuade his readers?
2. Why do you think he initially supported the "doctrine of gradual abolition"?

Angelina Grimké Tells the Truth

Angelina Grimké, the daughter of a slaveholder, was born in Charleston, South Carolina, in 1805. From a young age, she witnessed slaveholders' harsh treatment of the enslaved. She grew to hate the practice of slavery.

As young women, she and her sister, Sarah, moved north and vowed to speak out against the institution. In 1836, Angelina wrote a pamphlet titled *Appeal to the Christian Women of the South*, in which she called on Southern women to join the antislavery movement. Sarah wrote a similar work, addressed to clergy. Officials in South Carolina burned the pamphlets and warned the Grimké sisters that they would be arrested if they attempted to return to Charleston. The Grimkés' activities also drew criticism from men in the North. Many of them believed women shouldn't be involved in politics or even engage in public speaking. Unafraid, the sisters simply broadened the range of their activism to become advocates for women's rights. The following is a portion of Angelina Grimké's *Appeal to the Christian Women of the South.*

> It is through the tongue, the pen, and the press, that truth is principally propagated. Speak then to your relatives, your friends, your acquaintances on the subject of slavery; be not afraid if you are conscientiously convinced it is sinful, to say so openly, but calmly, and to let your sentiments be known. If you are served by the slaves of others, try to

ameliorate their conditions as much as possible; never aggravate their faults, and thus add fuel to the fire of anger already kindled ... Discountenance all cruelty to them, all starvation, all corporal chastisement; these may brutalize and break their spirits, but will never bend them to willing, cheerful obedience. If possible, see that they are comfortably and seasonably fed, whether in the house or the field; it is unreasonable and cruel to expect slaves to wait for their breakfast until eleven o'clock, when they rise at five or six. Do all you can, to induce their owners to clothe them well, and then allow them many little indulgences which would contribute to their comfort. Above all, try to persuade your husband, father, brothers, and sons, that slavery is a crime against God and man, and that it is a great sin to keep human beings in such abject ignorance; to deny them the privilege of learning to read and write ...

Some of you own slaves yourselves. If you believe slavery is sinful, set them at liberty, "undo the heavy burdens and let the oppressed go free." If they wish to remain with you, pay them wages, if not let them leave you. Should they remain teach them, and have them taught the common branches of an English education; they have minds and those minds ought to be improved.

—From Angelina E. Grimké, *Appeal to the Christian Women of the South* (New York: New York Anti-Slavery Society, 1836).

CONSIDER THIS

1. Do you think many Southern women followed Grimké's advice?
2. Grimké encourages women to teach enslaved people to read and write. Why were slaves kept in ignorance? Why do you think Grimké thought it was a "great sin" not to educate them?

Frederick Douglass: "This Fourth of July Is Yours, Not Mine"

Writer, abolitionist, and runaway, Frederick Douglass was a gifted orator, or speechmaker, who inspired and captivated his audiences. "I shall never forget his speech," recalled William Lloyd Garrison, who heard him at an antislavery convention. "I think I never hated slavery so intensely as at that moment."

Born into slavery, Douglass escaped in 1838, when he was about twenty years old. By the 1850s, he was traveling around the country giving lectures. His firsthand experience with slavery, his passionate language, and his powerful voice made him an effective advocate for emancipation.

On July 5, 1852, the Ladies Antislavery Society in Rochester, New York, asked Douglass to give a speech honoring the signing of the Declaration of Independence. Douglass agreed, but his words would take aim at the values and history that Americans held most sacred. "Fellow-citizens, pardon me, allow me to ask, why am I called upon to speak here to-day?" Douglass said to those gathered to hear him. "This Fourth of July is yours, not mine. You may rejoice, I must mourn." The following passage is from his famous speech.

As a young man, Douglass was an active abolitionist. He would go on to become a US government official and an advocate for both civil rights and women's rights.

> What, to the American slave, is your 4th of July? I answer: a day that reveals to him, more than all other days in the year, the gross injustice and cruelty to which he is the constant victim. To him, your celebration is a sham; your boasted liberty, an unholy license; your national greatness, swelling vanity; your sounds of rejoicing are empty and heartless; your denunciations of tyrants, brass fronted impudence; your shouts of

liberty and equality, hollow mockery; your prayers and hymns, your sermons and thanksgivings, with all your religious parade, and solemnity, are, to him, mere bombast, fraud, deception, impiety, and hypocrisy—a thin veil to cover up crimes which would disgrace a nation of savages.

There is not a nation on the earth guilty of practices, more shocking and bloody, than are the people of these United States, at this very hour ...

The existence of slavery in this country brands your republicanism as a sham, your humanity as a base pretence, and your Christianity as a lie. It destroys your moral power abroad; it corrupts your politicians at home. It saps the foundation of religion; it makes your name a hissing, and a by word to a mocking earth. It is the antagonistic force in your government, the only thing that seriously disturbs and endangers your Union.

—From Frederick Douglass, "What to the Slave Is the Fourth of July?" Reprinted in William L. Andrews, ed., *The Oxford Frederick Douglass Reader* (New York: Oxford University Press, 1997).

CONSIDER THIS

1. How does Douglass's use of the pronoun "your" help to make his point about how black people and white people view the Fourth of July differently?
2. What does he say the celebrations reveal about white Americans?

KEY TERMS AND CONCEPTS

From Frederick Douglass's speech:

antagonistic Actively oppressive.

bombast Language used to impress people that means little.

by word Byword, or a word or phrase that is frequently used, often in a mocking way.

denunciations Public statements of disapproval.

impiety A lack of religion.

pretence Pretense, or a false display.

From John Brown's address to the court:

validity The state of being officially binding.

John Brown's Insurrection

A white abolitionist named John Brown planned a raid on the armory, a place where military weapons are kept, in Harpers Ferry, Virginia (present-day West Virginia). He hoped that his actions would encourage slaves to join in the rebellion. He also hoped he would soon have a big enough army, as well as enough weapons from the armory, to fight for their emancipation.

On October 16, 1859, Brown put his plan into action. He and twenty-one men successfully seized the armory and held sixty people hostage. However, no slaves came to support him. The local militia and then the marines ultimately put an end to the insurrection, leaving ten of Brown's men dead, including two of his sons. Brown was captured, along with six others. Five managed to escape. The captives were quickly tried for insurrection, murder, and treason, or the crime of betraying the country. They were found guilty and sentenced to death.

At first, people were shocked by Brown's violent actions. Soon, however, many Northerners began to speak of him as a hero, especially after learning about his address to the court, quoted below. The insurrection, though not successful in the way Brown had hoped, is believed to have sped up the movement toward civil war and, ultimately, emancipation.

> The court acknowledges, as I suppose, the validity of the law of God. I see a book kissed here which I suppose to be the Bible ... That teaches me that all things whatsoever I would that men should do to me, I should do even so to them. It teaches me further to "remember them that are in bonds, as bound with them." I endeavored to act up to that instruction ... I believe that to have interfered as I have done—as I have always freely admitted I have done—in behalf of His despised poor, was not wrong, but right. Now if it is deemed necessary that I should forfeit my life for the furtherance of the ends of justice, and mingle my blood further with the blood of my children and with the blood of millions in this slave country whose rights are disregarded by wicked, cruel, and unjust enactments.—I submit; so let it be done!
>
> —From "Address of John Brown to the Virginia Court at Charles Town, Virginia" on November 2, 1859.

US marines stormed into the armory that John Brown captured in Harpers Ferry, bringing Brown's insurrection to an end. It would not, however, bring about the end of social unrest.

CONSIDER THIS

1. Brown refers to the Bible as justification for his actions. What biblical concept is he referring to?

The Dawn of War

The John Brown insurrection is just one example of how tensions between people who were for and against slavery bubbled over. During the 1850s, the interests of North and South would collide more violently than ever. Several events, including Brown's rebellion, brought about the arrival of what seemed inevitable: a war.

Bleeding Kansas was a period of violence between proslavery and antislavery advocates. They fought over the fate of slavery in the territory in the 1850s.

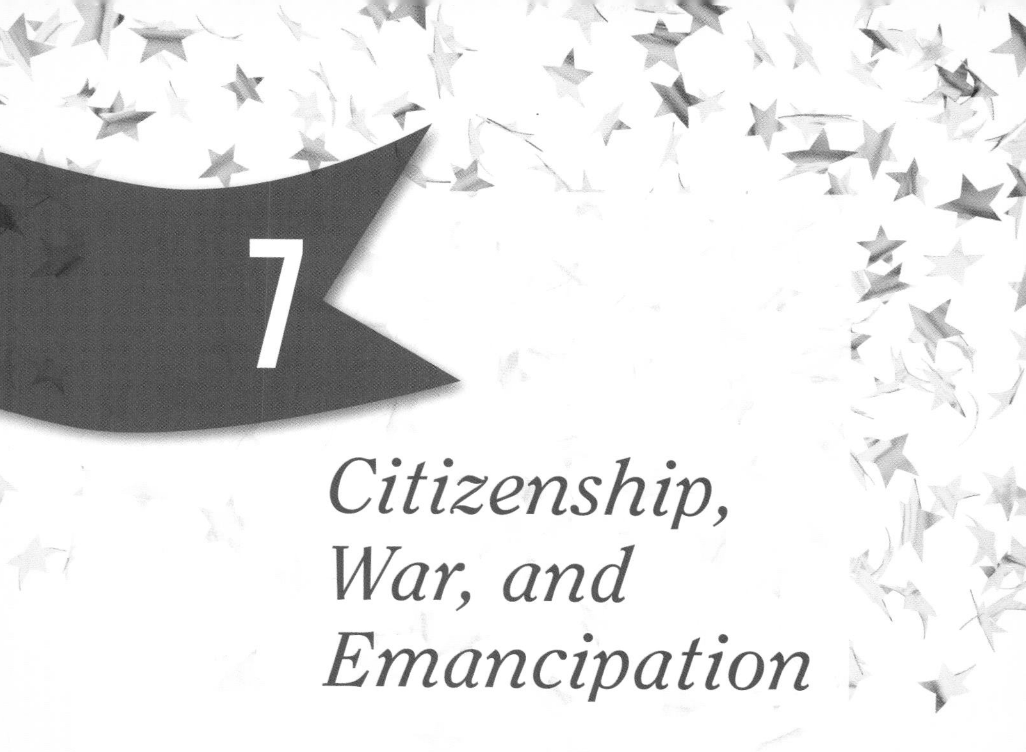

7

Citizenship, War, and Emancipation

In early 1854, Senator Stephen A. Douglas, a Democrat from Illinois, introduced the Kansas-Nebraska bill. After much debate, first in the Senate and then in the House, the bill was passed. The new law allowed these two territories—and any that came after—to enter the Union with or without slavery. The decision of whether to be a slave state or Free State would be reached by popular sovereignty, or decided by the vote of the people who lived there. At first, people in the North and South believed the law would help to lessen tensions. After all, it seemed democratic: the people would decide the issue for themselves. However, the Kansas-Nebraska Act did not ease hostility. It only ignited new tension.

Bleeding Kansas

Nebraska was too far north to attract many slaveholders. However, Kansas became a battleground between proslavery and antislavery forces. Groups on both sides began to rally supporters to settle in the territory. They hoped to tilt the territorial elections in their favor.

In March 1855, elections to the territory's legislature were held. Mobs of slaveholders from neighboring Missouri and Arkansas entered Kansas. They took over the polling places, drove the real settlers away from the polls, and cast their votes in favor of proslavery candidates. At the election's end, the number of ballots counted was almost double the number of settlers eligible to vote in Kansas.

Violence soon erupted. Proslavery groups destroyed the free soil town of Lawrence in 1856. In revenge, abolitionist John Brown killed five proslavery settlers in the region. This was three years before he led his insurrection at Harpers Ferry. These murders started a period of violent clashes known as Bleeding Kansas. The conflict would last until 1861.

Around the same time that the Bleeding Kansas conflict started, an enslaved man was suing for his freedom in Missouri. After the case went through several lower courts, the Supreme Court agreed to hear the case.

Slavery and Citizenship

In the 1830s, an enslaved man named Dred Scott lived in Missouri. His owner, Peter Blow, died, and Dr. John Emerson purchased Scott. Emerson was a doctor for the US Army. At different points in the 1830s, Dr. Emerson was sent to live in the Free State of Illinois and the Wisconsin Territory, where slavery was illegal. He took Scott with him. The army eventually ordered Emerson back to the South, and Scott returned to the slave state of Missouri.

Dred Scott and his wife, Harriet, fought for their freedom for over ten years before being denied both their freedom and citizenship in the United States by the Supreme Court.

In 1843, however, Emerson died. Scott became the property of Emerson's widow.

At some point, Scott learned that his extended stay in the Free States and territories meant he might be able to claim his freedom. In 1846, with the help of abolitionists, he sued for his freedom in court. He claimed he should be free because he had lived on free soil for a long time. After more than ten years of appeals, the case went all the way to the US Supreme Court. In March 1857, Scott lost the decision when the court declared that a black person, enslaved or free, could not be a US citizen. As a noncitizen, Scott had no rights and could not sue in a federal court. He, therefore, was not entitled to his freedom. The court's ruling had an impact on the lives of every black person in the United States. This decision took the nation one step closer to civil war.

The Rise of Abraham Lincoln

In 1858, a politician from Illinois was beginning to make a name for himself at the national level: Abraham Lincoln. He was the state's Republican candidate for the US Senate. He challenged Stephen Douglas—the incumbent, or the person currently holding the position—to a series of debates. The debate topics would include Kansas, the future of slavery, and the future of the Union itself.

Lincoln was a critic of slavery's spread. Meanwhile, Douglas was the author of the Kansas-Nebraska Act. The debates promised to be tense and dramatic. Journalists from all over the country came to observe and report. Although Lincoln lost the election, the debates made him famous. They made him so famous that the Republican Party selected him as its presidential candidate for the 1860 election. He won, with votes cast in his favor almost exclusively by Northerners. Less than two months later, before Lincoln had even taken office, South Carolina seceded from the Union.

The War Begins

Ten more Southern states followed South Carolina's example. Together, these eleven states formed the Confederate States of America. The decades-old threat of a nation divided had finally come to pass. By April 1861, the Civil War had begun. Four years of brutal conflict eventually led to a Northern victory. The North's triumph had many repercussions, but perhaps none was more critical than emancipation—an outcome of the war that would grant freedom to four million enslaved Africans.

The *Dred Scott* Decision

The *Dred Scott* case was heard by the Supreme Court in 1856. However, to many, it was clear that Scott had lost the case before the court ever considered it. Seven of the justices had been selected by proslavery presidents. Five of them came from slaveholding families. Their opinions were bound to be biased. The following court decision, written by Chief Justice Roger B. Taney, was announced in March 1857. Although he was morally opposed to slavery, he thought it was an issue that should be resolved by the states in which it existed. Additionally, he did not believe in racial equality.

> The question is simply this: Can a negro, whose ancestors were imported into this country, and sold as slaves, become a member of the political community formed and brought into existence by the Constitution of the United States, and as such become entitled to all the rights, and privileges, and immunities, guaranteed by that instrument to the citizen? One of which rights is the privilege of suing in a court of the United States in the cases specified in the Constitution …

We think they are not, and that [people of African origin] are not included, and were not intended to be included, under the word "citizens" in the Constitution, and can therefore claim none of the rights and privileges which that instrument provides for and secures to citizens of the United States. On the contrary, they were at that time considered as a subordinate and inferior class of beings …

They had for more than a century before [the Constitution was written] been regarded as … altogether unfit to associate with the white race, either in social or political relations; and so far inferior, that they had no rights which the white man was bound to respect; and that the negro might justly and lawfully be reduced to slavery …

And upon a full and careful consideration of the subject, the court is of opinion, that … Dred Scott was not a citizen of Missouri within the meaning of the Constitution of the United States, and not entitled as such to sue in its courts …

—From *Dred Scott v. Sandford*, March 6, 1857.

CONSIDER THIS

1. Did the court believe that Scott was entitled to bring a case to trial?
2. Why does the chief justice discuss how people of African origin were viewed at the time the Constitution was written?
3. According to the court, why wasn't Scott free?

KEY TERMS AND CONCEPTS

From the *Dred Scott* decision:
immunities Privileges.
subordinate Of a lower rank.

From Abraham Lincoln's speech:
agitation A state of anxiety.
augmented Increased.
avowed Publicly confessed.
ceased Stopped.

"A House Divided ... Cannot Stand"

Although Abraham Lincoln believed slavery was wrong, for most of his career he did not believe it should be abolished completely. He knew that any attempt to end slavery would seriously threaten the Union, so his goal was to keep the practice from spreading to new areas. However, Lincoln also began to fear that slavery might one day exist in every state. In June 1858, accepting the nomination as the Republican candidate for the US Senate, he gave a famous speech, an excerpt of which follows.

> We are now far into the fifth year since a policy [the Kansas-Nebraska Act] was initiated with the avowed object, and confident promise, of putting an end to slavery agitation. Under the operation of that policy, that agitation has not only not ceased, but has constantly augmented. In my opinion, it will

not cease, until a crisis shall have been reached and passed. "A house divided against itself cannot stand." I believe this government cannot endure permanently half slave and half free ... It will become all one thing, or all the other. Either the opponents of slavery will arrest the further spread of it, ... or its advocates will push it forward ...

—From Abraham Lincoln, "House Divided" Speech at Springfield, Illinois, June 16, 1858. Reprinted in Don E. Fehrenbacher, ed., *Abraham Lincoln: Speeches and Writings 1832–1858* (New York: Library of America, 1989).

CONSIDER THIS

1. What did Lincoln believe was the result of the Kansas-Nebraska Act?
2. What did he predict might happen in the future?

South Carolina's Declaration of Secession

Lincoln was elected president on November 6, 1860. By the end of the following month, South Carolina had seceded from the Union. The following year, most of the slave states would follow suit.

At his inauguration in March 1861, Lincoln urged the Confederates not to start a civil war. He said they had no right "to destroy the government, while I shall have the most solemn one to preserve, protect, and defend it." Despite what Lincoln said, Confederates attacked Fort Sumter, a Union fort off the coast of South Carolina, in April. The war began.

It would be the bloodiest war fought on US soil. Ultimately, it claimed the lives of more than six hundred thousand Americans. Some were fighting for constitutional principles and others for moral ideals. Some hoped to preserve states' rights and others to preserve the Union. The following is a selection from the South Carolina declaration of secession.

> The ends for which the Constitution was framed are declared by itself to be "to form a more perfect union, establish justice, insure domestic tranquility, provide for the common defence, promote the general welfare, and secure the blessings of liberty to ourselves and our posterity."
>
> These ends it endeavored to accomplish by a Federal Government, in which each State was recognized as an equal, and had separate control over its own institutions. The right of property in slaves was recognized by giving to free persons distinct political rights, by giving them the right to represent, and burthening them with direct taxes for three-fifths of their slaves; by authorizing the importation of slaves for twenty years; and by stipulating for the rendition of fugitives from labor.
>
> We affirm that these ends for which this Government was instituted have been defeated, and the Government itself has been made destructive of them by the action of the non-slaveholding States. Those States have assumed the right of deciding upon the propriety of our domestic institutions; and have denied the rights of property established in fifteen of the States and recognized by the Constitution; they have denounced as sinful the institution of slavery; they have permitted open establishment among them of societies, whose avowed object is to disturb the peace and to [take] the property of the citizens of

other States. They have encouraged and assisted thousands of our slaves to leave their homes; and those who remain, have been incited by emissaries, books and pictures to servile insurrection ...

A geographical line has been drawn across the Union, and all the States north of that line have united in the election of a man to the high office of President of the United States, whose opinions and purposes are hostile to slavery. He is to be entrusted with the administration of the common Government, because he has declared that that "Government cannot endure permanently half slave, half free," and that the public mind must rest in the belief that slavery is in the course of ultimate extinction ...

We, therefore, the People of South Carolina ... have solemnly declared that the Union heretofore existing between this State and the other States of North America, is dissolved, and that the State of South Carolina has resumed her position among the nations of the world, as a separate and independent State; with full power to levy war, conclude peace, contract alliances, establish commerce, and to do all other acts and things which independent States may of right do.

—From the South Carolina Declaration of Secession, December 1860.

KEY TERMS AND CONCEPTS

From South Carolina's declaration of secession:

burthening Burdening.

denounce To declare something as wrong.

emissary A representative.

incite To encourage.

levy To begin or wage (as in war).

propriety Properness.

stipulating for the rendition Demanding the surrender and return.

tranquility Peace or calm.

From the Thirteenth Amendment:

jurisdiction Authority.

CONSIDER THIS

1. Which parts of the Constitution does the declaration use to justify the decision to leave the Union? Is the argument it puts forth a logical one?
2. The declaration quotes Lincoln's "House Divided" speech. How do you think Southerners interpreted the quotation in light of Lincoln's election to the presidency?

A Proclamation that Changes the War's Focus

Lincoln never claimed that the war was being fought to free those who were enslaved. He was always focused on the preservation of the Union. As the war progressed, though, he saw reason to make a public statement concerning slavery. For one thing, more Northerners were turning against slavery. He no longer risked losing their significant support for the war. Additionally, he believed more European nations would help support the Union if he turned the focus toward slavery, as many European countries had already abolished slavery. Finally, many enslaved people were running away from their slave owners. As freedmen, they could join the Union army—something they might be more willing to do knowing that a Union victory would mean an end to slavery. With these factors in mind, Lincoln decided to issue the Emancipation Proclamation. As you read the excerpt here, keep in mind that four slaveholding states remained in the Union: Delaware, Kentucky, Maryland, and Missouri.

By the President of the United States of America:
A Proclamation.

Whereas, on the twenty-second day of September, in the year of our Lord one thousand eight hundred and sixty-two, a proclamation was issued by the President of the United States, containing, among other things, the following, to wit:

That on the first day of January, in the year of our Lord one thousand eight hundred and sixty-three, all persons held as slaves within any State or designated part of a State, the people whereof shall then be in rebellion against the United States, shall be then, thenceforward, and forever free ...

—From the Emancipation Proclamation,
January 1, 1863.

CONSIDER THIS

1. The Emancipation Proclamation frees only people enslaved in states "in rebellion against the United States." What does this mean?
2. Why didn't Lincoln free everyone that was enslaved?
3. Do you think many enslaved people were actually freed as a result of the Emancipation Proclamation? Why or why not?

Thirteenth Amendment Officially Ends Slavery

In the early years of the war, the Confederacy appeared to be winning. With exceptional military leadership, it won most of the battles. In 1863, however, the Union army saw more victories. By the beginning of 1865, the end of the war was in sight.

Lincoln turned his attention to putting an end to slavery in America forever. He took an active role in getting the Thirteenth Amendment to the US Constitution, the text of which appears below, passed. This amendment guaranteed the end of slavery in all of the states.

He also supported congressmen who insisted that at war's end, no Southern state could return to the Union without adopting the amendment. Although Lincoln looked forward to rebuilding the nation after the long, painful years of war, it was not to be. Five days after Confederate general Robert E. Lee surrendered to Union general Ulysses S. Grant, Lincoln was assassinated.

> AMENDMENT XIII
> Section 1.
> Neither slavery nor involuntary servitude, except as a punishment for crime whereof the party shall have been duly convicted, shall exist within the United States, or any place subject to their jurisdiction.
>
> Section 2.
> Congress shall have power to enforce this article by appropriate legislation.
>
> —The Thirteenth Amendment to the US Constitution, passed by Congress January 31, 1865; ratified December 6, 1865.

CONSIDER THIS

1. Why do you think the second section of the amendment was necessary? To what type of legislation might this refer?

The Post–Civil War South

What was life like for African Americans following the war? Had freedom greatly improved their lives? Certainly, freedom was better than bondage. Following the Thirteenth Amendment, two more amendments were passed that also held the promise of great change. The Fourteenth Amendment gave the rights of citizenship to all people who were born in the United States or who had undergone naturalization, or the process through which someone goes to obtain citizenship. This amendment effectively overturned the *Dred Scott* decision's assertion that African Americans could not be considered US citizens. The amendment also prohibited individual states from taking away a citizen's rights. The Fifteenth Amendment granted suffrage, or the right to vote, to black men. Women of all races would not be permitted to vote until 1920.

However, opinions among the majority of Southerners were not transformed by the events of the war, the Emancipation Proclamation, or the amendments to the Constitution. The South lay in ruins. The prejudice and ill will that had existed prior to the conflict were only intensified by the devastation it had caused.

The years following the war are known as the Reconstruction Era, generally considered to have lasted from 1865 to 1877. In those years, control of the South shifted between Southerners and Northerners. Initially, government remained in the hands of the same sorts of Southerners as the ones responsible for the war. However, Northerners took over by the end of 1867. They ran the governments of the South and worked to ensure the safety of the

This 1868 political cartoon depicts Oliver Otis Howard, the head of the Freedmen's Bureau, trying to maintain peace between white Southerners and African Americans.

former slaves. They established an agency, the Freedmen's Bureau, to help rebuild the South and protect black people.

Despite the bureau's efforts, the South continued to be a difficult place for black people. Colonel Samuel Thomas, an official working for the bureau, captured the sentiment of Southerners in one of his reports. He wrote:

> The reason of all this is simple and manifest. The whites esteem [consider] the blacks their property by natural right, and however much they may admit that the individual relations of masters and slaves have been destroyed by the war and the President's emancipation proclamation, they still have an ingrained feeling that the blacks at large belong to the whites at large, and whenever opportunity serves they treat the colored people just as their profit, caprice [mood] or passion may dictate.
>
> —From Colonel Samuel Thomas, Assistant Commissioner, Bureau of Refugees, Freedmen and Abandoned Lands, in 39 Cong., 1 Sess., Senate Exec. Doc. 2 (1865).

Despite the work of the Freedmen's Bureau, the South was a dangerous and uncertain place for African Americans by the late nineteenth century. Although they were granted citizenship and the right to vote, white Southerners stood in the way of them enjoying many of these privileges. Additionally, over time, the state governments would return to the hands of white Southerners.

In 1877, newly elected president Rutherford B. Hayes would withdraw the troops who were stationed in the South to protect the newly freed population. After that, it was unlikely that black people would be treated as equals in a land where they were once considered property. Southern states passed new state constitutions that strictly limited every aspect of African Americans' lives. These laws were only further reinforced by Supreme Court decisions.

In 1896, the Supreme Court ruled in *Plessy v. Ferguson* that the segregation, or separation, of train cars based on race was legal. This decision led to widespread segregation and a series of segregation-related policies known as Jim Crow laws. Although slavery had ended, new obstacles stood in the way of African Americans enjoying the full privileges of being citizens in the United States. The legacies of slavery and segregation continue to affect the treatment of African Americans in the United States today.

This 1940 image of a bus station in Durham, North Carolina, depicts how segregation extended to all parts of society, including waiting rooms.

CHRONOLOGY

1619 English pirates bring twenty Africans to Jamestown, Virginia, to be sold into slavery.

1705 A Virginia law declares that enslaved people are considered real estate.

1776 Thomas Jefferson writes the Declaration of Independence.

1787 The US Constitution is adopted by a convention of the states; it includes three sections that relate to slavery.

1789 The first slave narrative, *The Interesting Narrative of the Life of Olaudah Equiano*, is published.

1808 An act of Congress, passed the previous year, abolishes the slave trade.

1831 Nat Turner leads a slave rebellion in Southampton County, Virginia. Turner is captured and executed.

1850 The Compromise of 1850 establishes that slavery will be illegal in the new state of California and imposes strict punishments on anyone who helps runaways escape.

1854 Congress passes the Kansas-Nebraska Act, fueling violence and unrest in Kansas.

1857 The Supreme Court rules that no black person, enslaved or free, is a citizen of the United States (*Dred Scott v. Sandford*).

1859 John Brown seizes the armory in Harpers Ferry, Virginia.

1860 Abraham Lincoln is elected president. South Carolina is the first state to secede from the Union.

1861 Ten more states secede from the Union and form the Confederate States of America. The Civil War begins when the Confederates attack Fort Sumter.

1863 The Emancipation Proclamation becomes law on January 1.

1864 Lincoln is elected to a second term.

1865 In April, Confederate general Robert E. Lee surrenders at Appomattox Courthouse, Virginia, officially ending the Civil War, though fighting continues for months. In the same month, Lincoln is assassinated. The Thirteenth Amendment is ratified in December.

1868 The Fourteenth Amendment is ratified.

1870 The Fifteenth Amendment is ratified.

1877 President Rutherford B. Hayes pulls troops out of the South, effectively ending Reconstruction.

1896 The Supreme Court rules that segregation of train cars is legal (*Plessy v. Ferguson*).

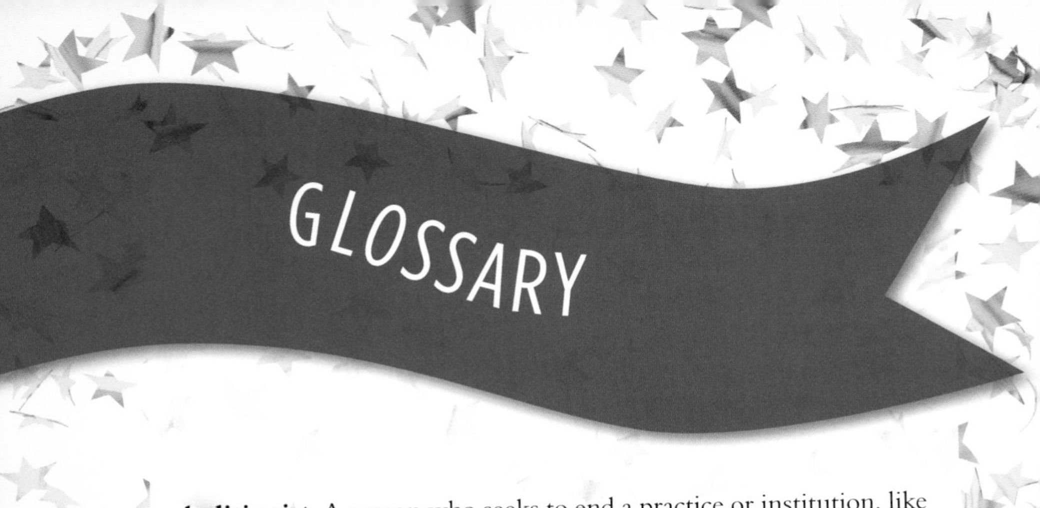

abolitionist A person who seeks to end a practice or institution, like slavery in the United States.

American Civil War A conflict (1861–1865) that broke out between the North and the South in the United States.

chattel A part of personal property, for instance a slave in pre–Civil War America.

Confederate States of America The established government (1861–1865) of the eleven states that seceded from the United States of America: in order of secession, South Carolina, Mississippi, Florida, Alabama, Georgia, Louisiana, Texas, Virginia, Arkansas, Tennessee, and North Carolina.

cotton gin A machine that separates the seeds, hulls, and other material from cotton.

emancipate To set someone free, especially from slavery.

Emancipation Proclamation A proclamation made by Abraham Lincoln, which freed everyone enslaved in the Confederacy.

excerpt A selection or quote from a longer body of work.

Fifteenth Amendment This amendment to the US Constitution, ratified in 1870, gives every male citizen the right to vote without regard to his "race, color, or previous condition of servitude."

Fourteenth Amendment This amendment to the US Constitution, ratified in 1868, guarantees citizenship to all people born in the United States. It guarantees citizens equal protection under the law and fair treatment by the court system.

free soil The idea that slavery would not expand into the western territories.

hold The part of a ship meant for cargo.

indentured servant A person who signed a contract to work for a person for a period of time, usually seven years, in exchange for something like room, board, or passage to the United States.

Kansas-Nebraska Act An 1854 law allowing Kansas and Nebraska to decide whether or not to be slave states by popular vote of their citizens.

quarantine To isolate a person or thing in an attempt to avoid spreading a contagious disease.

secede To formally withdraw from membership in a union or organization.

slave narrative An account of an enslaved person's life in bondage.

Thirteenth Amendment This amendment to the US Constitution, ratified in 1865, makes slavery illegal.

treason The crime of betraying one's country.

FURTHER INFORMATION

Books

Butler, Octavia. *Kindred: A Graphic Novel Adaptation.* New York: Abrams ComicArts, 2017.

David, Kenneth C. *In the Shadow of Liberty: The Hidden History of Slavery, Four Presidents, and Five Black Lives.* New York: Henry Holt and Company, 2016.

Edwards, Judith. *Fighting for Freedom: Abolitionists and Slave Resistance.* Slavery and Slave Resistance. New York: Enslow, 2016.

Morretta, Alison. *Slavery in Colonial America.* Primary Sources of Colonial America. New York: Cavendish Square Publishing, 2018.

Websites

Born in Slavery: Slave Narratives from the Federal Writers' Project, 1936 to 1938

https://www.loc.gov/collections/slave-narratives-from-the-federal-writers-project-1936-to-1938/about-this-collection

This website contains over 2,300 recorded slave narratives, like Richard Toler's and Tempe Herndon Durham's, that were recorded by the Federal Writers' Project.

National Geographic:
A History of Slavery in the United States
https://www.nationalgeographic.org/interactive/slavery-united-states

This interactive website provides a more detailed timeline concerning slavery in colonial America and the United States.

Slavery and the Making of America: Slave Memories
https://www.thirteen.org/wnet/slavery/memories/index_flash.html

This website has audio recordings from those who survived slavery and the Reconstruction Era, along with photos of life in the nineteenth century.

Videos

Dawn of Day: Stories from the Underground Railroad
https://www.youtube.com/watch?v=L5c6cDCTJNY

This documentary explores Bleeding Kansas and the Underground Railroad in Wabaunsee County, Kansas.

The Evolution of Slavery in Colonial America:
The African Americans
https://wvia.pbslearningmedia.org/resource/mr13.socst.us.slaverycolonialva/the-evolution-of-slavery-in-colonial-virginia/#.Wx55XC3MzdQ

This short video, from a longer series called The African Americans: Many Rivers to Cross, explores the progression of how black people were treated in colonial Virginia.

Organizations

Getting Word: African American Families of Monticello
931 Thomas Jefferson Parkway
Charlottesville, VA 22902
(434) 984-9800
Website: https://www.monticello.org/getting-word

This oral history project records the oral histories of descendants of those enslaved at Monticello, Thomas Jefferson's home and plantation.

The Legacy Museum:
From Enslavement to Mass Incarceration,
and the National Memorial for Peace and Justice
115 Coosa Street
Montgomery, Alabama 36104
(334) 386-9100
Website: https://museumandmemorial.eji.org

Run by the Equal Justice Initiative, this museum and memorial are focused on slavery and its legacy in the United States. They are located in Montgomery, Alabama, near the site of "one of the most prominent slave auction spaces in America."

National Museum of African American
History and Culture
1400 Constitution Ave NW
Washington, DC 20560
(202) 633-1000
Website: https://nmaahc.si.edu

The museum's Slavery and Freedom exhibit provides a powerful representation of the lives of enslaved Africans. It also discusses the effects of the institution of slavery in exhibits like Defending Freedom, Defining Freedom.

National Underground Railroad Freedom Center
50 East Freedom Way,
Cincinnati, OH 45202
(513) 333-7500
Website: http://www.freedomcenter.org

This museum and education center provides visitors with history about slavery, the Civil War, and the Underground Railroad, while also highlighting stories of those who still fight for freedom today.

The Slave Dwelling Project
P.O. Box 1469
Ladson, SC 29456
Website: http://slavedwellingproject.org

This organization works to identify and preserve slave quarters. They also offer lectures, living history presentations, and overnights in existing slave quarters to help further illuminate the lives enslaved Africans led.

The Whitney Plantation
5099 Highway 18
Wallace, LA 70049
(225) 265-3300
Website: http://whitneyplantation.com

This museum provides visitors with the opportunity to learn about the lives of enslaved people in Louisiana through the museum's exhibits and first-person slave narratives.

INDEX

Page numbers in **boldface** refer to images.

ABOUT THE AUTHORS

Chet'la Sebree is a writer, editor, and researcher from the Mid-Atlantic. She has received degrees in English and writing from the University of Richmond and American University. She has worked on several books about US history, including the Courting History series for Cavendish Square Publishing. Her research focus is early American history and slavery at Monticello, Thomas Jefferson's plantation.

Elizabeth Sirimarco published her first book in 1990. Since that time, she has written books on a range of topics such as Thomas Jefferson and the Cold War. A graduate of the University of Colorado at Boulder, she also earned a degree in Italian from the Università per Stranieri in Siena, Italy. In addition to writing, Sirimarco works as an editor and occasionally enjoys the opportunity to work as an Italian translator. She and her husband David, a photographer, live with a very large dog and a very small cat in Denver, Colorado.